DOLOMI...

TRAVEL GUIDE

2024-2025

**Explore Majestic Peaks, Hiking
Trails, Cultural Experiences,
Activities, Accommodation and
Practical Tips for an Unforgettable
Italian Mountain Escape.**

JASON H. FORD

TABLE OF CONTENTS

INTRODUCTION

Welcome to the Dolomites, a region where nature's grandeur meets cultural richness and history whispers through every stone and trail. Situated in the northern Italian Alps, the Dolomites are renowned for their breathtaking landscapes, towering peaks, and idyllic villages that seem to spring from a fairy tale. This is a place where the natural beauty of rugged mountain ranges and serene alpine lakes merges with a vibrant cultural tapestry and fascinating historical legacy. It is a destination that promises adventure, tranquility, and a deep connection with nature.

My journey to these majestic peaks was sparked by a thirst for adventure and a desire to immerse myself in one of Europe's most stunning natural settings. From the moment I first gazed upon the jagged, snow-capped peaks that seemed to touch the sky, I knew I was in for an extraordinary experience.

Arriving in the picturesque town of Cortina d'Ampezzo, known as the "Queen of the Dolomites," was the perfect starting point for my adventure. I stayed at a charming mountain lodge that offered incredible views of the surrounding peaks and immediate access to some of the region's best outdoor activities. Cortina's blend of luxury and rustic charm set the stage for an exhilarating exploration of the Dolomites.

One of my most unforgettable experiences was hiking the Tre Cime di Lavaredo loop. This iconic trail offered stunning views of the three distinctive peaks and the lush alpine meadows below. The thrill of navigating the rugged terrain and the awe-inspiring vistas made it a truly memorable adventure. Another highlight was an afternoon at Lago di Braies. The lake's turquoise waters, framed by towering mountains, created a scene of such pristine beauty that it felt like stepping into a fairytale. Renting a rowboat and gliding across the tranquil waters was a serene yet exhilarating experience that perfectly captured the spirit of the Dolomites.

But the Dolomites offer more than just spectacular landscapes. The region is steeped in culture and history, with charming alpine villages that reveal the traditional Ladin way of life. Sampling local delicacies like speck and canederli, and participating in vibrant festivals in villages like San Cassiano, added a rich cultural layer to my adventure. Each experience deepened my connection to the region and enhanced the thrill of discovery.

In this guide, you'll find detailed information on the best hiking routes, where to stay, and how to dive into the local culture. I've included personal anecdotes from my travels to help you feel more engaged with the region and offer practical advice based on firsthand experience. Whether you're planning a week-long adventure or a weekend getaway, this guide aims to make your trip to the Dolomites as exciting and memorable as possible.

So, as you turn the pages of this guide, imagine yourself embarking on your own adventure—scaling mountain peaks, exploring hidden trails, and experiencing the vibrant local culture. I hope this guide inspires you to set out on your own journey and create unforgettable memories in this breathtaking corner of Italy.

Overview of the Dolomite Region

The Dolomites, located in the northern Italian Alps, are a stunning mountain range celebrated for their dramatic peaks, serene valleys, and picturesque landscapes. Covering parts of the provinces of Belluno, South Tyrol, and Trentino, the Dolomites span over 141,903 hectares and are recognized as a UNESCO World Heritage site. This region is characterized by its unique geological formations, diverse climate, and rich cultural heritage.

Geographically, the Dolomites are distinguished by their jagged, pale-colored peaks formed from dolomitic limestone. These peaks, such as the iconic Tre Cime di Lavaredo and the imposing Marmolada, the highest peak at 3,343 meters, create a striking contrast against the lush green valleys and forests below. The region boasts numerous crystal-clear lakes, cascading waterfalls, and scenic meadows, making it a paradise for nature lovers and outdoor enthusiasts.

The climate in the Dolomites varies significantly with altitude and season. Summers are generally mild and pleasant, with temperatures ranging from 15°C to 25°C, ideal for hiking, cycling, and exploring the outdoors. Winter brings cold temperatures, often dropping below freezing, and significant snowfall, transforming the region into a winter wonderland perfect for skiing, snowboarding, and other winter sports. Spring and autumn offer a mix of mild and cool temperatures, with fewer tourists, providing a tranquil and picturesque setting for visitors.

One of the most unique characteristics of the Dolomites is the phenomenon known as "enrosadira" or "alpenglow." During sunrise and sunset, the pale dolomitic rocks take on a spectacular reddish hue, creating a breathtaking display of colors that attract photographers and nature enthusiasts from around the world.

In addition to its natural beauty, the Dolomites are a cultural mosaic. The region is home to a blend of Italian, Ladin, and German-speaking communities, each with its own distinct traditions, languages, and cuisines. This cultural diversity is reflected in the local festivals, architecture, and culinary delights, offering visitors a rich and immersive experience.

The Dolomites are also renowned for their outdoor activities. In the warmer months, the region becomes a haven for hikers, climbers, and cyclists, with numerous trails and routes catering to all levels of experience. During winter, the Dolomites' ski resorts, such as Cortina d'Ampezzo and Val Gardena, draw winter sports enthusiasts from around the globe. The region's natural parks, like the Dolomiti Bellunesi National Park and the Puez-Odle Nature

Park, provide ample opportunities for wildlife spotting and eco-tourism.

The Dolomites are a region of extraordinary natural beauty, diverse climate, and rich cultural heritage. From its dramatic mountain peaks and serene lakes to its vibrant cultural traditions and outdoor adventures, the Dolomites offer a unique and captivating destination for travelers seeking both relaxation and adventure.

Why You Should Visit the Dolomites

The Dolomites, a stunning range of mountains in northern Italy, have long captivated travelers with their otherworldly beauty and rich cultural heritage. This majestic region continues to offer unparalleled experiences for those seeking adventure, relaxation, and a deep connection with nature. Here's why you should consider the Dolomites as your next travel destination:

1. Breathtaking Natural Beauty

The Dolomites are renowned for their dramatic landscapes, characterized by towering peaks, deep valleys, and serene alpine lakes. The Dolomites remain a haven for nature lovers, with their rugged terrain offering some of the most picturesque views in Europe. Whether you're marveling at the iconic Three Peaks (Tre Cime di Lavaredo), exploring the pastel-hued cliffs of the Cinque Torri, or enjoying the tranquil beauty of Lago di Braies, the scenery is simply breathtaking. The Dolomites' unique rock formations, shaped over millions of years, provide a constantly changing panorama that promises to leave you in awe.

2. World-Class Hiking and Outdoor Activities

For outdoor enthusiasts, the Dolomites are a paradise. The region continues to offer an extensive network of hiking trails suitable for all levels of experience. From gentle walks through lush meadows to challenging climbs on rugged peaks, there's a trail for every adventurer. The Alta Via 1, a renowned long-distance trek, provides an immersive journey through the heart of the mountains. Additionally, the Dolomites offer excellent opportunities for skiing, snowboarding, and mountain biking, ensuring year-round excitement for those seeking adrenaline-pumping activities.

3. Rich Cultural and Historical Heritage

The Dolomites are not just about natural beauty; they also boast a rich cultural tapestry. The region is home to the Ladin people, whose unique language and traditions have been preserved for centuries. Visitors can experience the charm of traditional Ladin culture through local festivals, artisan crafts, and authentic cuisine. The architecture in towns like Ortisei and San Cassiano reflects a blend of alpine charm and historical influences, offering a glimpse into the region's past. Don't miss the opportunity to visit historical sites such as the World War I fortifications, which add a poignant layer to the region's historical narrative.The open-air museums and restored tunnels, such as those at Lagazuoi and

Marmolada, offer a poignant glimpse into the past and the hardships faced by soldiers in this harsh terrain.

4. Culinary Delights

The Dolomites are a haven for food lovers. The region's cuisine is a delightful fusion of Italian and Austrian influences, featuring hearty, comforting dishes that reflect the mountainous environment. In 2024, you can savor local specialties such as speck (cured ham), canederli (bread dumplings), and strudel. The emphasis on locally sourced ingredients ensures that every meal is a fresh and flavorful experience. Dining in the Dolomites also offers the added pleasure of enjoying your meal with stunning mountain views, creating a memorable culinary experience.

5. Warm Hospitality and Unique Accommodations

The Dolomites are renowned for their warm and welcoming hospitality. Visitors can choose from a range of accommodations that cater to various preferences and budgets. Whether you prefer a luxury spa hotel with panoramic mountain views, a cozy family-run guesthouse, or a charming alpine chalet, the options are plentiful. The hospitality in the Dolomites is characterized by genuine warmth and a commitment to ensuring a memorable stay, making you feel like part of the local community.

Dolomites offer a captivating blend of natural beauty, outdoor adventure, cultural richness, and culinary delights. This remarkable region continues to be a must-visit destination for travelers seeking a unique and unforgettable experience. From its awe-inspiring landscapes and diverse activities to its rich cultural heritage and warm hospitality, the Dolomites promise to leave a lasting impression on every visitor.

Brief History and Culture of the Dolomites

The Dolomites, a striking mountain range in northern Italy, are not only renowned for their breathtaking landscapes but also for their rich historical and cultural heritage. The region's history is as layered and intricate as its geological formations, shaped by a diverse mix of peoples, traditions, and events over the centuries.

Historical Background

The Dolomites, part of the Southern Limestone Alps, have been formed over millions of years through a complex process of geological activity. The region's unique rock formations, known for their pale color and distinctive shapes, are the result of ancient coral reefs that once existed here. These formations are a testament to the area's deep geological past, with the most prominent peaks rising sharply against the skyline, creating a dramatic and awe-inspiring landscape.

Throughout history, the Dolomites have been a strategic location due to their position between the Italian Peninsula and Central Europe. During the Roman Empire, the area was relatively remote and sparsely inhabited, serving as a natural barrier and a haven for local tribes. The region's history took a significant turn during the Middle Ages when it became part of the Austrian-Hungarian Empire. The influence of this empire is still evident in the architecture and cultural practices found in the Dolomite region today.

In the 20th century, the Dolomites played a pivotal role during World War I, as the rugged terrain became a battleground between Italian and Austro-Hungarian forces. Many of the fortifications and trenches from this period are still visible and offer a poignant reminder of the area's wartime history. The reconstruction of the region after the war led to a renewed focus on tourism, which has since grown to become a major part of the local economy.

Cultural Heritage

The cultural heritage of the Dolomites is equally rich and diverse, shaped by its geographical location and historical influences. The region is home to several distinct ethnic groups, including the Ladin people, who speak a Romance language unique to the area. The Ladin culture is a vital part of the Dolomites' identity, characterized by its own language, traditional music, and folklore. The Ladin people have preserved their cultural practices over centuries, maintaining a strong sense of community and tradition.

Traditional Ladin architecture is notable for its charming wooden chalets and intricately carved facades, which blend seamlessly with the natural environment. Many villages in the Dolomites, such as Ortisei and San Cassiano, showcase this traditional architecture, offering visitors a glimpse into the region's past. These villages also host local festivals that celebrate traditional crafts, music, and cuisine, providing an immersive cultural experience.

The cuisine of the Dolomites reflects its cultural melting pot, with influences from both Italian and Austrian traditions. Local specialties include hearty dishes like speck (cured ham), canederli (bread dumplings), and strudel. The culinary heritage is deeply tied to the land, with many dishes featuring locally sourced ingredients and traditional cooking methods.

The Dolomites are also renowned for their festivals and cultural events, which offer a vibrant celebration of the region's heritage. The annual festival of San Lorenzo in San Cassiano, for example, is a lively event featuring traditional music, dance, and local cuisine. These festivals not only provide a glimpse into the local customs but also serve as a gathering point for residents and visitors alike.

In summary, the Dolomites are a region steeped in history and culture, offering a fascinating blend of natural beauty and rich heritage. From its ancient geological formations and historical significance to its vibrant Ladin culture and traditional festivals, the Dolomites provide a captivating backdrop for any traveler eager to explore and experience its unique character.

CHAPTER 1
PLANNING YOUR TRIP

When to Visit

The Dolomites offer a distinct experience throughout the year, each season bringing its own set of features and attractions. Understanding the best times to visit based on weather, events, and local festivals can greatly enhance your trip.

In spring, from April to June, the Dolomites emerge from winter with blooming wildflowers and melting snow. Temperatures during this period range from 10°C to 20°C, providing comfortable weather for hiking and exploring. Rainfall is moderate, and the landscapes come alive with color as meadows and valleys are covered in a blanket of blossoms. Key events in spring include the Festa di San Marco on April 25, which celebrates St. Mark with parades and local festivities, and the South Tyrol Jazz Festival in late June, featuring jazz performances in scenic and unique settings.

Summer, from July to September, is the peak tourist season. Temperatures typically range from 15°C to 25°C, and the weather is generally warm and sunny, with occasional afternoon thunderstorms. This season is ideal for outdoor activities such as hiking, climbing, and cycling. The Maratona dles Dolomites, held in early July, is a major cycling event attracting participants from around the world, while the Südtirol Classic Schenna in July showcases vintage cars along picturesque routes.

Autumn, from October to November, offers a quieter experience with cooler temperatures between 5°C and 15°C. The fall foliage transforms the region into a vibrant display of reds, oranges, and yellows. Rainfall is moderate, and the first snow falls may appear in November. The Speckfest in October celebrates South Tyrolean speck (cured ham) with tastings and local crafts, and Törggelen, from October to November, is a harvest festival featuring new wine, roasted chestnuts, and regional dishes.

Winter, from December to March, turns the Dolomites into a snowy paradise, perfect for winter sports. Temperatures often drop below freezing, and the region is covered with heavy snowfall. This season is renowned for its skiing, snowboarding, and snowshoeing opportunities. The Christmas markets in December, held in towns like Bolzano and Bressanone, offer a festive atmosphere with crafts and seasonal treats, while the Ski World Cup, also in December, attracts top skiers to compete in thrilling races.

The peak tourist seasons in the Dolomites are during the summer months (July to September) and the winter ski season (December to March). These times can be crowded, and accommodation prices may be higher. For a more peaceful visit, consider the shoulder seasons of spring and autumn.

Participating in local festivals and events can enhance your travel experience by providing insight into the region's culture and traditions. Whether you are drawn to vibrant summer activities, serene autumn landscapes, or winter sports, each season in the Dolomites offers unique opportunities for exploration and enjoyment.

Essential Packing List

When preparing for a trip to the Dolomites, packing appropriately for the season and activities you plan to enjoy is crucial. Each season in the Dolomites presents its own set of weather conditions and opportunities, so tailoring your packing list to match can make a significant difference in your experience. Here's a detailed guide to ensure you're well-prepared for your adventure.

In spring, the weather can be unpredictable with a mix of mild temperatures and occasional rain. For this season, bring layered clothing that can adapt to changing conditions. Lightweight waterproof jackets are essential to stay dry during unexpected showers. Sturdy hiking boots with good grip are a must for exploring the trails as they can get muddy. Don't forget a hat and sunglasses for sunny days, as well as a daypack for carrying essentials like water, snacks, and a camera.

Summer in the Dolomites is warm and sunny, but temperatures can vary depending on the altitude. Pack light, breathable clothing for daytime activities, along with a few warmer layers for cooler evenings. A high-quality sunscreen is essential to protect your skin from the strong alpine sun. A good pair of hiking boots or trail shoes will serve you well for exploring the numerous trails, and a wide-brimmed hat can help shield you from the sun. Don't forget to bring a reusable water bottle to stay hydrated during your adventures.

Autumn brings cooler temperatures and beautiful fall foliage. Layered clothing is key, as mornings and evenings can be chilly while daytime temperatures are more moderate. A warm, insulated jacket and a hat will help keep you comfortable. Waterproof clothing is still important, as rain showers are common. Good hiking boots are still necessary for walking on potentially slippery trails, and a pair of gloves may come in handy for the crisp mornings. A camera with extra memory cards is ideal for capturing the stunning autumn scenery.

Winter in the Dolomites means cold temperatures and plenty of snow. Pack heavy-duty winter clothing including insulated jackets, thermal layers, and snow proof pants. Waterproof and windproof outerwear is crucial for staying warm and dry. Sturdy, waterproof boots with good insulation will keep your feet warm and dry on snowy trails. Don't forget ski gear if you plan on hitting the slopes, including skis, poles, and goggles, or if you're renting, make sure you have proper fitting gear. Warm gloves, a hat, and thermal socks are essential for protection against the cold.

On my own trip to the Dolomites, I once forgot to pack a crucial item: my hiking boots. I had planned an ambitious hike in the Dolomiti di Sesto and ended up having to make do with a pair of regular sneakers. The experience was far from ideal as the trails were muddy and rocky, and my sneakers offered little support or traction. The discomfort made the hike much less enjoyable and served as a harsh reminder of how important it is to pack the right gear for the activities you plan to undertake. Since then, I've made it a point to double-check my packing list to ensure I don't leave anything crucial behind.

By tailoring your packing list to the season and activities, you'll be better prepared to fully enjoy the wonders of the Dolomites.

Traveling to the Dolomites on a Budget

Exploring the Dolomites doesn't have to break the bank. With a little planning, you can enjoy the natural beauty, rich culture, and vibrant local life of this stunning region without spending a fortune. From budget-friendly accommodations to cost-effective dining and affordable activities, here's how you can make the most of your Dolomite adventure on a budget.

When it comes to accommodation, the Dolomites offer several budget-friendly options that don't sacrifice comfort or location. Hostels are a great choice for travelers looking to save money while meeting fellow adventurers. In towns like Bolzano and Cortina d'Ampezzo, you can find clean and well-equipped hostels that provide a social atmosphere and convenient amenities. Guesthouses and family-run bed and breakfasts offer a more intimate and often more affordable alternative to hotels. These establishments frequently provide homemade breakfasts and local insights that enhance your stay. For those preferring hotels, consider options in smaller towns or on the outskirts of major tourist areas, where prices are generally lower but still offer easy access to main attractions.

Dining on a budget in the Dolomites is entirely feasible while still allowing you to savor authentic local cuisine. Local markets are perfect for picking up fresh produce, cheeses, and cured meats, which can be enjoyed as picnic meals. Food trucks and street vendors in towns like Ortisei and San Candido offer delicious, inexpensive street food, ranging from hearty sandwiches to sweet treats. For a more sit-down experience, look for trattorias and pizzerias that serve generous portions at reasonable prices. These eateries often feature regional specialties and provide a true taste of local flavors without the higher costs of tourist-oriented restaurants.

There are also plenty of free or low-cost activities that allow you to immerse yourself in the Dolomites' natural beauty and cultural richness. Many of the region's parks and nature reserves, such as the Fanes-Senes-Braies Nature Park, have minimal entrance fees and offer extensive hiking trails with breathtaking views. Scenic viewpoints, like those at the Lago di Braies or the Alpe di Siusi, provide stunning vistas that are perfect for photography and relaxation. Cultural events, such as local festivals and markets, often have free admission and offer a glimpse into traditional customs and community life. Visiting historic villages and wandering through charming streets can also be a delightful and cost-free way to experience the area's culture and history.

During one of my budget trips to the Dolomites, I stayed at a charming guesthouse in a small village outside of Cortina d'Ampezzo. The host provided delicious homemade breakfasts and offered great advice on local hikes and affordable dining spots. I made the most of local markets for my meals and discovered a delightful food truck offering amazing local dishes at a fraction of the cost of restaurant meals. One particularly memorable experience was exploring the trails around Lago di Braies, where the stunning natural beauty was completely free to enjoy and provided a perfect backdrop for a picnic made from market finds.

Traveling on a budget in the Dolomites doesn't mean missing out on any of the region's remarkable experiences. With a bit of creativity and local knowledge, you can enjoy comfortable accommodations, delicious food, and unforgettable activities without stretching your wallet. Embrace the charm of budget travel, and you'll find that the Dolomites offer a wealth of experiences that are both enriching and affordable.

Visa and Entry Requirements

Traveling to the Dolomites, which are part of Italy, requires understanding and preparing for the visa and entry requirements. For international travelers, these requirements vary based on your nationality and the purpose of your visit. Here's a detailed guide to ensure a smooth entry into this beautiful region.

First, check whether you need a visa to enter Italy. Citizens of European Union (EU) and Schengen Area countries do not require a visa for short stays of up to 90 days. For travelers from other countries, including the United States, Canada, Australia, and many others, a short-stay visa may be required if you plan to stay longer than 90 days or if your country does not have visa-free agreements with Italy.

If a visa is required, you will need to apply for a Schengen visa, which allows entry into Italy and other Schengen countries. The application process involves several steps. Begin by scheduling an appointment with the Italian consulate or embassy in your home country. Prepare the necessary documents, including a valid passport with at least two blank pages and a validity of at least three months beyond your planned departure date from the Schengen Area. You will also need to provide proof of travel insurance that covers medical expenses and repatriation for the duration of your stay.

Additional documents typically include proof of accommodation in the Dolomites, such as hotel reservations or an invitation letter from a host, as well as proof of sufficient financial means to cover your stay. This could be recent bank statements or a letter from your employer. You should also be prepared to submit a detailed itinerary of your travel plans and possibly a return ticket or proof of onward travel.

When applying for a visa, it's important to apply well in advance of your travel date. The processing time can vary, so allowing at least 15 days to several weeks is advisable. Ensure that all documents are complete and accurate to avoid delays or issues with your application.

For travelers not requiring a visa, it's still important to ensure that your passport is valid for the duration of your stay and complies with any entry requirements. You may be asked to show proof of onward travel or sufficient funds to support your stay, so having these documents readily available can make your entry process smoother.

Another key aspect to consider is customs regulations. Italy has specific rules regarding the importation of goods, such as limits on the amount of alcohol and tobacco products you can bring into the country. Familiarize yourself with these regulations to avoid any issues upon arrival.

As you prepare for your trip, keep in mind that entry requirements can change, so it's wise to check the latest information from official sources, such as the Italian embassy or consulate, well before your departure. Having the correct documents and understanding the entry requirements will ensure a hassle-free start to your adventure in the Dolomites.

Travel Tips for a Smooth Journey

Traveling to the Dolomites can be a memorable experience, and being well-prepared will help ensure a smooth and enjoyable journey. Here are some practical travel tips, including insights into local customs and etiquette, to help you make the most of your trip.

Start by familiarizing yourself with the local customs and etiquette. Italians are known for their warm hospitality, but they also value politeness and formality. When greeting someone, a handshake is the most common form of greeting, though close friends and family might greet each other with a hug or a kiss on both cheeks. In more formal settings, such as when meeting someone for the first time, a handshake is appropriate.

Dress modestly, especially when visiting religious sites such as churches or monasteries. It is customary to cover your shoulders and avoid wearing shorts or revealing clothing in these places. In restaurants and more upscale venues, Italians tend to dress neatly and stylishly, so consider wearing smart-casual attire for dining out.

When it comes to dining, be aware of local dining customs. Italians typically eat their meals at specific times: lunch is usually served from 12:30 PM to 2:30 PM, and dinner starts around 7:30 PM or later. Many restaurants might not open for dinner until 7:00 PM, so plan accordingly. Tipping is not mandatory but is appreciated, and rounding up the bill or leaving a small amount is a common practice.

Learn a few basic Italian phrases, even if you're not fluent. Simple greetings like "Buongiorno" (Good morning) or "Grazie" (Thank you) can go a long way in making a positive impression and showing respect for the local culture. While many people in the Dolomites speak English, especially in tourist areas, making an effort to speak Italian will be appreciated.

Be mindful of the local pace of life. Italians often value a relaxed approach to life and may take their time with service. This can be a pleasant change from the fast-paced environment you might be used to, so take the opportunity to relax and enjoy your surroundings.

In terms of practical travel tips, ensure you have a copy of your passport, travel insurance details, and any important documents in a secure location separate from the originals. It's also wise to carry some cash, as smaller establishments may not accept credit cards. The local currency is the Euro, and ATMs are widely available.

When driving in the Dolomites, be aware that roads can be narrow and winding. Take your time, drive cautiously, and be prepared for varying weather conditions. It's also helpful to have a GPS or a reliable map, as some areas might not have clear road signs.

Understanding and respecting local customs, preparing for practical aspects of your journey, and embracing the relaxed Italian lifestyle, you'll be well-equipped to enjoy everything the Dolomites have to offer. Your trip will be enriched by these thoughtful preparations, allowing you to fully appreciate the beauty and culture of this stunning region.

Accommodation Options

The Dolomites offer a range of distinctive accommodations that capture the region's unique character and natural beauty. Whether you're looking for a touch of luxury, a sustainable stay, or a dive into local history, these options provide memorable experiences tailored to different preferences.

For a taste of elegance and local charm, consider staying at Hotel Lago di Braies. Situated by the picturesque Lago di Braies, this boutique hotel combines rustic alpine style with modern comforts. Address: Strada Statale 51, 39030 Braies, Italy. To get there, drive from the nearest town, Brunico, taking the SS49 and then the SS51. This hotel features stunning lake views, beautifully appointed rooms, and a spa with wellness treatments. Prices typically range from 150 to 300 euros per night, depending on the season. It's ideal for travelers seeking a luxurious retreat with easy access to scenic hiking and boating opportunities.

Another notable boutique hotel is the Grand Hotel Savoia in Cortina d'Ampezzo. Address: Via Roma 82, 32043 Cortina d'Ampezzo, Italy. It's located in the town center, making it convenient to explore local shops and restaurants. This grand hotel offers elegant rooms, a full-service spa, and a gourmet restaurant. Prices generally range from 200 to 400 euros per night. It's perfect for travelers who appreciate classic luxury and want to experience the sophisticated side of the Dolomites.

For those who prioritize sustainability, the Eco-Hotel Zhero in Ischgl is a top choice. Address: Hnr. 53, 6561 Ischgl, Austria. Located just across the border from Italy, the hotel is accessible by taking the A13 motorway to the Ischgl exit. This eco-lodge features energy-efficient design, organic toiletries, and locally sourced food. The hotel also offers a wellness area with a sauna and relaxation rooms. Rates typically range from 120 to 250 euros per night. It's an excellent option for eco-conscious travelers who want to stay close to nature while minimizing their environmental impact.

Another eco-friendly choice is Hotel & Bio Restaurant Kesselberg in La Villa. Address: Str. Plan da Tieja 10, 39036 La Villa, Italy. Located in the heart of the Dolomites, it's easily reached by driving from the town of San Cassiano via the SS244. This eco-lodge uses sustainable practices and offers organic meals sourced from local farms. The hotel's amenities include a wellness area with a sauna and panoramic mountain views. Prices range from 100 to 200 euros per night. This accommodation suits travelers who are passionate about sustainability and enjoy a tranquil, nature-focused experience.

For a more historical ambiance, stay at Albergo Posta Marcucci in Bagno Vignoni. Address: Via della Storia 1, 53027 Bagno Vignoni, Italy. To reach this historic inn, drive from Siena via the SS2 and then the SR2. The inn offers a unique blend of traditional Tuscan décor with modern comforts. It features an extensive spa with thermal baths, reflecting the town's historic use of thermal springs. Room rates usually range from 130 to 250 euros per night. This inn is perfect for travelers interested in history and relaxation.

The Hotel al Lago in San Candido provides another historic experience. Address: Via Dolomiti 5, 39038 San Candido, Italy. It's located in the heart of the town, making it convenient for exploring local shops and restaurants. The hotel is housed in a historic building with traditional alpine design and offers comfortable, quaint rooms. Prices generally range from 80 to 150 euros per night. It's ideal for travelers who want to experience local culture and history in a cozy, family-run setting.

These accommodations each offer a unique way to experience the Dolomites. Whether you're seeking luxury, sustainability, or historical charm, these options cater to a range of preferences and provide a memorable stay in this breathtaking region.

CHAPTER 2
GETTING TO THE DOLOMITES.

Choosing the Best Flights

Reaching the Dolomites begins with selecting the right flight, and there are several major airlines that offer direct flights to airports near this stunning region. For travelers flying from international destinations, the most convenient airports are Venice Marco Polo Airport (VCE) and Innsbruck Airport (INN). Venice Marco Polo, located approximately 160 kilometers from the Dolomites, is served by airlines such as Alitalia, Lufthansa, and easyJet. Innsbruck Airport, situated around 90 kilometers away, is serviced by carriers like Austrian Airlines and Swiss International Air Lines.

When booking your flight to the Dolomites, finding the best deals can significantly enhance your travel experience. One effective strategy is to book your flight well in advance. Airlines often release promotional fares months ahead of departure, and booking early can help you secure a better price. Flexibility with travel dates is another valuable tip. Flying on weekdays or during off-peak seasons can lead to lower fares. Using price comparison websites, such as Skyscanner or Google Flights, allows you to compare prices across multiple airlines and find the best deals.

When traveling to the Dolomites, it's important to be aware of airport fees, taxes, and baggage restrictions. Most airlines will include airport taxes in the ticket price, but it's wise to check for any additional fees related to checked baggage or seat selection. Standard baggage policies often allow one carry-on bag and one checked bag, but this can vary by airline. Make sure to review the baggage rules before your journey to avoid extra charges. Additionally, some airports may have small service fees for amenities or services, which are generally modest but worth noting.

Reflecting on my own journey to the Dolomites, I recall a memorable adventure that began with a somewhat unexpected detour. I had booked a flight to Venice Marco Polo with a plan to travel by train to my final destination. However, a sudden snowstorm in Venice led to flight delays and re-routing through Munich. What initially seemed like a setback turned into an impromptu exploration of Munich's beautiful winter streets and cozy cafés. By the time I finally reached the Dolomites, the experience had added an unexpected layer of adventure to my trip, reminding me of the serendipitous joys of travel.

Understanding these aspects of your flight journey can help you prepare effectively and minimize surprises along the way. With careful planning and a bit of flexibility, you can ensure a smooth start to your adventure in the Dolomites, allowing you to focus on enjoying the breathtaking landscapes and rich experiences that await you.

Local Transportation: Buses and Cable Cars

Navigating the Dolomites is a breeze with the region's efficient and well-connected local transportation options, particularly buses and cable cars. These modes of transport are not only practical but also offer unique ways to experience the stunning landscapes.

The local bus system in the Dolomites is extensive and reliable, connecting major towns and popular tourist spots. Companies like Südtirol Bus and Dolomiti Bus operate routes throughout the region, providing access to key destinations such as Cortina d'Ampezzo, Ortisei, and Val Gardena. Buses are well-maintained and comfortable, offering scenic views along the way. Routes are designed to cater to both residents and tourists, with schedules that accommodate daily commutes and sightseeing trips. During the peak tourist season, buses run more frequently to manage the increased demand, making it easier to get around even during busy periods.

Purchasing bus tickets is straightforward. You can buy them at bus stations, newsstands, or sometimes directly from the driver. For travelers planning to use public transport extensively, there are also travel passes available that offer unlimited rides for a set period, which can be a cost-effective option. These passes often include discounts or additional benefits, such as reduced rates for local attractions.

Cable cars and gondolas are another essential aspect of local transportation in the Dolomites, offering not only convenience but also breathtaking views of the mountains. These cable cars provide access to higher altitudes and are a popular choice for reaching ski resorts or hiking trails. For instance, the Lagazuoi Cable Car, near Cortina d'Ampezzo, offers a quick ascent to high-altitude trails and ski areas, with panoramic views of the surrounding peaks. The Dolomiti Superski area features a network of gondolas and cable cars that link various ski resorts, making it easy to explore different parts of the region without the hassle of driving.

Using cable cars can be a highlight of your visit, as they offer a unique perspective of the Dolomites from above. Tickets for cable cars can be purchased at the base stations or online in advance, and prices vary depending on the route and duration of the ride. Many cable cars also offer combined tickets that include access to multiple attractions or areas, providing added convenience for those planning to explore extensively.

Both buses and cable cars in the Dolomites are well-integrated, making it easy to transfer between different modes of transport. This seamless connectivity ensures that you can travel comfortably and efficiently while taking in the stunning scenery of this beautiful region. Whether you're heading to a remote hiking trail or moving between charming towns, these local transportation options enhance your experience and make exploring the Dolomites both enjoyable and practical.

Driving in the Dolomites: Tips and Routes

Driving in the Dolomites offers a unique opportunity to explore the region at your own pace, but it requires some preparation due to the mountainous terrain and varying road conditions. Here are some detailed tips to ensure a smooth driving experience, along with recommendations for scenic routes.

The roads in the Dolomites are well-maintained, but they can be narrow and winding, particularly in the more remote areas. It's important to drive cautiously, especially if you are not accustomed to mountainous driving. Ensure your vehicle is in good condition, as sharp turns and steep inclines can put extra strain on the engine and brakes. Winter tires are essential during the colder months, and snow chains may be required if road conditions become particularly challenging. Check local regulations and weather conditions before setting out.

One of the most popular scenic routes is the Great Dolomite Road (Grande Strada delle Dolomiti), which stretches from Bolzano to Cortina d'Ampezzo. This route offers stunning views of the Dolomite peaks and passes through charming villages such as Ortisei and Canazei. Along the way, you'll encounter several viewpoints and landmarks, making it a great option for a leisurely drive.

Another must-drive route is the Sella Ronda, a circular route around the Sella Massif. This loop is renowned for its breathtaking landscapes and is especially popular among skiers in the winter. The drive provides panoramic views of the surrounding mountains and is a fantastic way to appreciate the grandeur of the Dolomites.

The Passo delle Erbe is another scenic drive worth exploring. This pass connects the Val Badia and the Val di Funes valleys and offers dramatic vistas of the peaks and alpine meadows. It's a quieter route compared to the more popular passes, providing a more serene driving experience.

When driving through the Dolomites, be prepared for varying weather conditions. Even in summer, sudden weather changes can occur, leading to fog, rain, or even snow at higher elevations. Keep an eye on weather forecasts and road conditions, and drive according to the conditions. Road signs are generally clear, but be aware of signs indicating switchbacks and steep gradients.

Parking can be limited in popular tourist areas, so it's a good idea to plan your parking arrangements in advance. Many towns and resorts have designated parking areas, and in some cases, parking fees may apply. It's also worth noting that some areas are restricted to traffic during peak hours, so be sure to check local regulations and times for any restrictions.

In summary, driving in the Dolomites can be a rewarding experience with the right preparation. By taking note of road conditions, driving cautiously, and exploring scenic routes, you'll be able to fully appreciate the natural beauty and charm of this remarkable region. Whether you're navigating winding roads or enjoying panoramic views, driving in the Dolomites will offer you a memorable and immersive experience.

Guided Tours and Excursions

Making the most of your visit.

The Dolomites offer a variety of tour packages that cater to different interests and travel styles. Whether you prefer guided tours, self-guided walking tours, or adventure excursions, there are options available to enhance your experience in this stunning region. Here's a detailed look at some of the tour packages you can explore, including their duration, cost, and what they offer.

Guided tours in the Dolomites provide an informative and immersive way to explore the region. One popular option is the "Dolomite Highlights Tour," which typically lasts between 7 to

10 hours. This tour covers major sights such as the Sella Pass, Lago di Braies, and Cortina d'Ampezzo. The cost usually ranges from 80 to 150 euros per person, depending on the season and inclusions. These tours often include transportation in a comfortable vehicle, a knowledgeable guide, and sometimes lunch or refreshments. This package is ideal for families and couples who want a comprehensive overview of the Dolomites' most iconic landmarks without the hassle of planning logistics.

For those who prefer a more personalized experience, private guided tours are available. These tours can be customized based on your interests, such as photography, local culture, or outdoor activities. Duration can vary from half a day to a full day, with prices generally starting around 200 euros for a half-day tour. Inclusions typically cover transportation, a private guide, and tailored experiences based on your preferences. Private tours are well-suited for couples and solo adventurers who seek a more intimate and flexible exploration of the Dolomites.

Self-guided walking tours offer a more independent way to explore the region, allowing you to set your own pace while following a detailed itinerary. These tours usually come with a map, route descriptions, and points of interest. One popular self-guided tour is the "Tre Cime di Lavaredo Loop," a classic hike that takes approximately 4 to 6 hours to complete. The cost for a self-guided walking tour package is generally between 30 and 60 euros and includes the necessary materials for navigation and trail information. This option is ideal for solo adventurers and couples who enjoy exploring at their own pace and prefer a more active experience.

Adventure excursions in the Dolomites cater to those looking for a more adrenaline-filled experience. The "Dolomite Adventure Package" might include activities such as rock climbing, via ferrata (protected climbing routes), or mountain biking. These excursions typically last from half a day to a full day, with prices ranging from 100 to 300 euros per person. Inclusions often cover equipment rental, professional guides, and safety instructions. This package is best suited for adventure enthusiasts and thrill-seekers who want to challenge themselves and experience the Dolomites from a different perspective.

Another exciting option is the "Winter Sports Excursion," which includes skiing or snowboarding in popular resorts such as Val Gardena or Cortina d'Ampezzo. These excursions generally last a full day, with prices starting around 120 euros per person, including lift passes, equipment rental, and a guide or instructor. This package is perfect for families and couples who enjoy winter sports and want to experience the best slopes and facilities in the Dolomites.

The Dolomites offer a range of tour packages to suit various interests and travel styles. Whether you prefer guided tours, self-guided walks, or adventure excursions, each package provides a unique way to experience the beauty and excitement of the region. Choosing the right tour depends on your preferences and travel companions, ensuring that you make the most of your visit to this breathtaking destination.

CHAPTER 3
EXPLORING THE DOLOMITES

Overview of the Dolomite Mountain Range

The Dolomites are a remarkable mountain range located in northeastern Italy, known for their dramatic peaks, lush valleys, and unique geological significance. Formed over 200 million years ago from ancient coral reefs, the Dolomites are characterized by their distinctive pale-colored rock formations, which give the mountains their unique appearance and name. This region is a UNESCO World Heritage site, celebrated for its breathtaking natural beauty and rich geological history.

The Dolomites' limestone and dolomite rock formations create sharp, vertical cliffs, spires, and pinnacles, making it one of the most picturesque mountain ranges in the world. The landscape is further enhanced by expansive alpine meadows, crystal-clear lakes, and dense forests. The contrast between the rugged peaks and the verdant valleys creates a striking visual effect that captivates visitors from all over the globe.

One of the most notable features of the Dolomites is the phenomenon known as enrosadira, or alpenglow.

During sunrise and sunset, the mountains take on a magical pink and orange hue, a result of the unique mineral composition of the rock. This natural light show is a highlight for many visitors and adds to the mystical allure of the region.

I remember a hike I took in the Dolomites that truly showcased the stunning landscapes of this region. It was a crisp autumn morning when I set out on the Tre Cime di Lavaredo trail, one of the most famous hikes in the Dolomites. The trail is known for its panoramic views and relatively moderate difficulty, making it accessible to most hikers. As I began my ascent, the early morning light bathed the towering peaks in a warm, golden glow, enhancing their rugged beauty.

The trail wound through alpine meadows, where the last of the summer wildflowers were still in bloom, creating a vibrant contrast against the backdrop of gray and white rock. I passed several serene lakes, their waters reflecting the towering peaks above. The air was fresh and crisp, filled with the scent of pine and the occasional call of a mountain bird.

As I reached the higher elevations, the views became even more spectacular. The three distinctive peaks of Tre Cime di Lavaredo loomed majestically ahead, their sharp silhouettes etched against the clear blue sky. Standing at the foot of these colossal formations, I felt a profound sense of awe and connection to the natural world. The sheer scale and beauty of the Dolomites were truly humbling.

The descent offered equally stunning vistas, with the changing light casting different shadows and highlights on the mountains. By the time I returned to the trailhead, the sun was beginning to set, and the enrosadira phenomenon painted the peaks in soft pink and orange hues. It was a perfect end to a day filled with natural wonder and unforgettable scenery.

The Dolomites are more than just a collection of beautiful mountains; they are a testament to the Earth's geological history and a paradise for nature lovers. Whether you are an avid hiker, a photographer, or simply someone who appreciates the beauty of the natural world, the Dolomites offer an unparalleled experience that will leave a lasting impression.

Unique Dolomitic Limestone Formations

The limestone formations of the Dolomites are not only visually striking but also of great geological significance. These formations, made primarily of dolomite rock, were created over millions of years from ancient coral reefs and marine sediments. Unlike other limestone formations, dolomite rock is known for its distinctive, often pale-colored hues and its resistance to weathering, which has resulted in the creation of sharp peaks, deep valleys, and dramatic cliffs.

One of the most iconic dolomitic formations is the Tre Cime di Lavaredo, or the Three Peaks of Lavaredo. These three towering spires dominate the landscape, standing out prominently against the sky. Their sheer, vertical walls and rugged silhouettes are a testament to the unique geological processes that shaped them. The Tre Cime are not just a geological marvel but also a cultural symbol of the Dolomites, frequently depicted in photographs and artworks.

During one of my visits, I had the chance to explore the Seceda Ridge, a formation known for its striking, almost surreal vertical cliffs. As I approached, the cliffs seemed to rise out of the earth like massive, sculpted monoliths. The distinctive, layered appearance of the dolomite rock was particularly captivating as it caught the afternoon light. The contrast between the pale rock and the vibrant green meadows at its base created a mesmerizing visual effect. Standing there, surrounded by the towering cliffs and expansive views, I felt a deep appreciation for the geological forces that had shaped this extraordinary landscape.

Stunning Lakes and Waterfalls

The Dolomites are home to some of Italy's most stunning lakes and waterfalls, each offering its own unique charm and natural beauty. Among the must-visit lakes is Lago di Braies, often referred to as the "Pearl of the Dolomites." This alpine lake is renowned for its crystal-clear waters, which mirror the surrounding peaks and forested slopes. The lake's tranquil setting, with its vibrant turquoise waters and the backdrop of the rugged mountain range, makes it a perfect spot for relaxation and reflection.

One memorable day I spent at Lago di Braies stands out vividly in my mind. It was early summer, and the lake was surrounded by lush greenery and blooming wildflowers. I rented a small rowboat and drifted across the lake, marveling at the reflection of the surrounding peaks in the still water. The serene atmosphere and the gentle lapping of the water against the boat provided a sense of calm and rejuvenation. After a leisurely row, I took a walk along the lakeside trail, which offered different perspectives of the lake and its stunning surroundings. The experience was not only visually captivating but also deeply restorative, providing a perfect escape into nature.

Another gem in the Dolomites is the Cascate di Fanes, a series of picturesque waterfalls nestled in the Val di Fanes. These waterfalls cascade down the rocky terrain, creating a soothing symphony of rushing water. The surrounding area is lush and green, adding to the sense of tranquility. I visited the Cascate di Fanes on a crisp autumn day, when the vibrant fall colors enhanced the beauty of the waterfalls. I spent several hours exploring the area, sitting by the base of the falls, and enjoying the invigorating mist and the sound of the cascading water. It was a truly refreshing experience, offering both physical and emotional renewal amidst the natural splendor.

Both the lakes and waterfalls of the Dolomites are not just beautiful landmarks; they are integral parts of the region's natural landscape, offering moments of peace and connection with the environment. Whether you're gazing at the serene waters of Lago di Braies or feeling the cool spray of the Cascate di Fanes, these natural features provide a profound sense of wonder and rejuvenation.

Flora and Fauna: Nature's Wonders

The Dolomites are a treasure trove of unique flora and fauna, offering a rich tapestry of plant and animal life that thrives in this diverse alpine environment. The region's varied elevations and microclimates create habitats for a wide array of species, each adapted to the specific conditions of the mountains.

In terms of flora, the Dolomites boast a remarkable range of plant life. At lower elevations, you'll find lush meadows adorned with wildflowers such as edelweiss, alpine roses, and gentians. As you ascend, the vegetation shifts to hardy alpine plants like lichens, mosses, and dwarf pines. The changing colors of the flora throughout the seasons add to the region's dynamic beauty, with spring bringing vibrant blooms and autumn showcasing a stunning array of fall colors.

The Dolomites are also home to a variety of fauna. The region's wildlife includes mammals such as chamois, ibex, and marmots, which are well-adapted to the mountainous terrain. Birds like the golden eagle and the alpine chough can be spotted soaring high above the peaks, while smaller creatures such as the snow vole and the mountain hare inhabit the lower altitudes.

One memorable wildlife encounter I had in the Dolomites occurred during a hike in the Val Gardena. As I was making my way along a remote trail, I heard a rustling in the underbrush nearby. Curious, I paused to investigate and was delighted to see a family of marmots emerging from their burrows. The marmots, with their round faces and curious expressions, were bustling about, collecting food and chattering among themselves. They seemed completely unbothered by my presence, allowing me to observe them up close.

The sight of these charming creatures in their natural habitat was both exhilarating and heartwarming. Their playful behavior and the way they interacted with one another provided a glimpse into the daily life of alpine wildlife. It was a reminder of the delicate balance of nature and the importance of preserving these pristine environments.

The flora and fauna of the Dolomites are integral to the region's allure, offering visitors a chance to connect with nature in a profound way. Whether you're admiring the vibrant wildflowers, spotting elusive wildlife, or simply enjoying the serene beauty of the natural surroundings, the Dolomites provide an enriching experience that celebrates the wonders of the natural world.

CHAPTER 4
REGIONS AND TOWNS

Trentino: Heart of the Dolomites

Situated in the northern part of Italy, is a region that embodies the essence of the Dolomites. Known for its breathtaking landscapes and charming towns, Trentino offers a diverse array of experiences that cater to nature lovers, history enthusiasts, and those seeking a tranquil escape.

Overview of Trentino

Trentino's natural beauty is a marvel in itself, with dramatic mountain ranges, serene lakes, and picturesque valleys. The region is dominated by the rugged peaks of the Dolomites, which provide a stunning backdrop for various outdoor activities. The towering mountains, such as the Pale di San Martino and the Brenta Dolomites, offer some of the best hiking and climbing opportunities in Europe. Trails like the Sentiero delle Bocchette offer exhilarating routes with panoramic views, while the well-marked paths around the Adamello-Presanella massif are ideal for more leisurely walks.

In winter, Trentino transforms into a paradise for skiing and snowboarding, with renowned resorts like Madonna di Campiglio and Val di Fassa drawing winter sports enthusiasts from around the world. For those who prefer mountain biking, the region offers an extensive network of trails that cater to all skill levels, providing thrilling rides through scenic landscapes.

Beyond the mountains, Trentino is home to serene lakes such as Lago di Tovel and Lago di Molveno. Lago di Tovel, known for its striking red-colored water in certain seasons, is surrounded by lush forests and is a peaceful spot for a day of relaxation. Lago di Molveno, with its crystal-clear waters and scenic surroundings, is perfect for a quiet afternoon by the water or a leisurely paddle in a rented boat.

Must-Visit Towns and Villages

Trentino is dotted with charming towns and villages that each offer their own unique experiences. Bolzano, the provincial capital, is a vibrant city known for its blend of Italian and Germanic cultures. The city's historical center is home to the South Tyrol Museum of Archaeology, where the famous Iceman, Ötzi, is displayed. Bolzano also offers a lively market scene and beautiful architecture, including the Gothic-style Bolzano Cathedral.

Trento, another key town in Trentino, is known for its historical and cultural significance. The city is home to the Trento Cathedral and the Buonconsiglio Castle, which provide insights into the region's medieval past. Trento also hosts the annual Christmas market, which is renowned for its festive atmosphere and artisanal crafts.

Riva del Garda, located on the northern tip of Lake Garda, is a picturesque town with a delightful lakeside setting. The town is known for its charming old town, historic fortifications, and the stunning views of the surrounding mountains. Riva del Garda is also a popular base for water sports and outdoor activities.

During a trip to Trentino, I had the pleasure of discovering the quaint village of Molveno. Nestled at the foot of the Brenta Dolomites, Molveno is a picturesque spot with a serene lake that reflects the surrounding peaks. I arrived in Molveno on a crisp autumn day, and the vibrant colors of the leaves created a stunning contrast against the clear blue sky.

Exploring the village, I met several locals who were friendly and eager to share their knowledge about the area. One memorable encounter was with a local artisan who crafted beautiful wooden carvings inspired by the Dolomites. He invited me to his workshop, where I learned about traditional woodcraft techniques and saw firsthand the artistry that went into his work.

The highlight of my visit was a peaceful afternoon spent by Lake Molveno. I rented a small boat and paddled across the lake, taking in the breathtaking views of the mountains reflected in the water. The experience was deeply rejuvenating, providing a perfect escape from the hustle and bustle of daily life.

Trentino's cultural and historical richness adds to its charm. In Molveno, the annual Lake Molveno Festival celebrates local traditions with music, food, and folk performances. Historical landmarks such as the Church of Saint Vigilio and the old village houses provide a glimpse into the region's past.

Practical Tips
When exploring Trentino, consider renting a car for the flexibility to explore remote areas and scenic drives. Accommodation options range from cozy guesthouses to luxury hotels, catering to various budgets. For dining, local trattorias offer hearty mountain cuisine, including dishes like speck, polenta, and apple strudel.

In addition to well-known attractions, Trentino offers unique experiences such as visiting local markets, where you can find artisanal cheeses, cured meats, and handcrafted goods. The region's small villages often have hidden gems, including charming cafes and picturesque viewpoints that offer a more intimate connection to Trentino's culture and landscape.

Trentino is a region that captures the essence of the Dolomites with its stunning landscapes, charming towns, and rich cultural heritage. Exploring this beautiful area offers a blend of natural beauty and historical intrigue, enhanced by personal experiences and local encounters. Whether you're hiking through the mountains, relaxing by a serene lake, or discovering the local culture, Trentino promises a memorable and enriching journey.

South Tyrol: A Cultural Mosaic

South Tyrol, a region in northern Italy, is a remarkable blend of Italian and Austrian influences that come together to form a unique and vibrant cultural landscape. This area, with its striking geographical location at the crossroads of two distinct cultures, has developed a rich and multifaceted identity that is evident in its architecture, traditions, and daily life.

The cultural identity of South Tyrol is deeply rooted in its historical and geographical context. Historically, South Tyrol was part of the Austro-Hungarian Empire until the end of World War I, when it was annexed by Italy. This transition has had a profound impact on the region's cultural landscape. The architectural styles reflect this heritage, with traditional Tyrolean wooden houses and Alpine chalets complementing the Italianate buildings found in towns such as Bolzano and Merano.

The region's cultural fusion is evident in many aspects of daily life. German and Italian are both widely spoken, and local customs and traditions often blend elements from both cultures. For example, you'll find Italian cuisine and German beer coexisting seamlessly in local restaurants and festivals. Traditional celebrations, such as Christmas markets and local fairs, often feature a mix of Austrian and Italian elements, creating a distinctive and engaging experience for visitors.

Major Attractions
South Tyrol is home to several key attractions that reflect its rich cultural mosaic. Bolzano, the capital, is known for its historical charm and cultural landmarks. The South Tyrol Museum of Archaeology is a highlight, showcasing Ötzi the Iceman, a remarkably preserved prehistoric mummy discovered in the Alps. This museum offers a fascinating look into the ancient past of the region.

Merano, another significant town, is celebrated for its elegant spa culture and beautiful architecture. The town's thermal baths and botanical gardens provide a relaxing retreat, while its historic buildings and Art Nouveau architecture offer a glimpse into its past. The annual Merano WineFestival is a notable event that attracts visitors from around the world, highlighting the region's renowned wine and culinary scene.

One of my most memorable experiences in South Tyrol was attending the "Törggelen" festival in a small village near Bolzano. This traditional autumn festival celebrates the end of the grape harvest and is marked by feasting, music, and the enjoyment of new wine. The festival was a sensory delight, with the aroma of roasted chestnuts and freshly baked bread filling the air, and lively folk music providing a festive soundtrack. Interacting with the locals, who were eager to share their traditions and stories, added a personal touch to the experience. This festival not only deepened my appreciation for South Tyrol's cultural blend but also created lasting memories of a vibrant and welcoming community.

To fully immerse yourself in South Tyrol's cultural environment, consider engaging in activities that allow you to experience local traditions firsthand. Participating in workshops, such as those focusing on traditional crafts or cooking, provides insight into the region's heritage. Visiting artisan shops where local craftspeople create unique items or attending cultural performances can also offer a deeper connection to the local culture.

The culinary scene in South Tyrol is a true reflection of its cultural fusion. Dishes such as speck (cured ham), apple strudel, and Tyrolean dumplings are staples of the local cuisine. Markets like the Bolzano Christmas Market offer a chance to sample these delicacies and explore local specialties. Dining at traditional restaurants or "Gasthäuser" will give you a taste of the region's rich culinary heritage, where Italian and Austrian flavors come together in delightful ways.

Tips
When traveling to South Tyrol, renting a car is often the best way to explore the region's diverse landscapes and attractions. Public transportation is also available and can be convenient for visiting larger towns and cities. Accommodations range from charming guesthouses to luxurious hotels, catering to various preferences and budgets. It's helpful to familiarize yourself with local etiquette, such as greeting people with a friendly "Grüß Gott" in German or "Buongiorno" in Italian, and to be mindful of the region's bilingual nature.

Engaging with local residents or cultural experts can provide additional insights into South Tyrol's unique cultural landscape. Locals are often enthusiastic about sharing their knowledge of regional traditions and hidden gems. For instance, exploring lesser-known villages or attending local events not widely advertised can reveal aspects of South Tyrol's culture that are off the beaten path.

South Tyrol's cultural richness and diversity offer a captivating blend of Italian and Austrian influences. By exploring its historical landmarks, participating in local festivals, and immersing yourself in its culinary and cultural experiences, you can gain a profound appreciation for this unique region. South Tyrol invites you to discover its vibrant cultural mosaic and create memorable experiences that reflect its distinctive heritage.

Belluno: Gateway to Adventure

Belluno, a picturesque city nestled in the Veneto region of northern Italy, is not just a gateway to the Dolomites but a destination in its own right. Its charm lies in its blend of historical significance, vibrant local culture, and proximity to some of the most stunning natural landscapes in the region.

Belluno has a rich history that stretches back to Roman times, and its role as a gateway to the Dolomites has shaped much of its character. The city's historical landmarks reflect its storied past and architectural evolution. The Belluno Cathedral, with its impressive façade and serene interior, stands as a testament to the city's historical depth. The Piazza dei Martiri, a central square lined with historical buildings and bustling cafes, serves as the heart of the city, offering a glimpse into Bellino's vibrant community life.

Key Attractions

The nearby Dolomiti Bellunesi National Park is a major draw for outdoor enthusiasts. This expansive park features rugged mountains, lush forests, and crystal-clear lakes, making it ideal for hiking, climbing, and nature photography. Trails such as the Tre Cime di Lavaredo offer breathtaking views of the iconic peaks that define the Dolomites. The park's diverse landscapes provide opportunities for various activities, from leisurely walks to challenging climbs.

In Belluno itself, local events and markets highlight the city's cultural spirit. The weekly market in Piazza dei Martiri showcases local crafts, fresh produce, and regional delicacies. Festivals such as the "Festa della Madonna del Carmine" celebrate traditional Italian culture with processions, music, and local cuisine.

One of my most memorable adventures from Belluno was a challenging hike through the Dolomiti Bellunesi National Park. Setting out early in the morning, I ventured along the rugged trails of the park, which offered a mix of challenging ascents and breathtaking vistas. The highlight of the hike was reaching a remote alpine lake, where the still waters perfectly reflected the surrounding peaks. The solitude and beauty of the lake provided a serene contrast to the demanding trek. Along the way, I encountered a local guide who shared fascinating insights into the region's geology and flora, enriching the experience even further.

Belluno served as a perfect base for this adventure. Its central location made it easy to access the park's trailheads. I stayed in a charming local guesthouse that provided comfortable accommodations and helpful advice on nearby hikes. For those planning a similar adventure, I recommend booking a local guide who can offer expert knowledge and ensure a safe and enjoyable experience. The journey to the trailheads was straightforward, with well-marked roads and ample parking available.

This adventure deepened my appreciation for Belluno and its surrounding landscapes. The challenge of the hike and the reward of the stunning views reinforced the city's role as a gateway to extraordinary natural experiences. The sense of accomplishment and connection with nature made the trip memorable, highlighting the region's potential for outdoor enthusiasts.

Tips
When planning a trip to Belluno, consider the best times for outdoor activities. Spring and autumn offer mild temperatures and fewer crowds, ideal for hiking and exploring. Summer can be busy, but it provides the opportunity for extended daylight hours and a wider range of activities. Winter, while colder, is perfect for those interested in skiing or snowboarding.

Accommodations in Belluno range from cozy guest houses to upscale hotels. It's advisable to book in advance, especially during peak seasons. Local amenities include outdoor gear rental shops and visitor centers where you can gather information and advice on local trails and activities.

Prepare for outdoor adventures by bringing appropriate gear, including sturdy hiking boots, weather-appropriate clothing, and plenty of water. Safety is paramount in the Dolomites, so ensure you are familiar with the trails and local conditions. Some areas may require permits or have specific regulations, so check in advance.

For an authentic adventure experience, consult local experts or guides who can provide insider knowledge and recommendations. Local adventure guides often know hidden trails and less-visited spots that offer unique experiences away from the crowds.

Belluno serves as an ideal gateway to the adventure-filled landscapes of the Veneto region. Its historical charm, coupled with its proximity to the Dolomites, makes it a perfect base for exploring the natural beauty and outdoor opportunities of the area. By embracing Belluno's unique blend of culture and adventure, travelers can uncover a wealth of experiences that highlight the region's distinctive character.

Notable Towns and Villages: Hidden Gems to Explore

Venture beyond the familiar sights and uncover the lesser-known towns and villages that offer a unique and authentic glimpse into the region's rich tapestry. These hidden gems, often overshadowed by their more popular counterparts, present opportunities for genuine discovery and connection.

Hidden Gems Overview

The region is home to several charming, lesser-known towns and villages that often escape the radar of mainstream tourism. One such town is Canazei, nestled in the heart of the Val di Fassa. With its traditional alpine architecture and vibrant local culture, Canazei offers a quintessential mountain experience. The town is renowned for its picturesque setting, with cozy chalets and stunning views of the surrounding peaks.

Another hidden gem is Ortisei, located in the Val Gardena. Ortisei is celebrated for its artisanal heritage, particularly its wood carving tradition. The town's narrow streets are lined with quaint shops selling beautifully handcrafted wooden souvenirs, and its central square, Piazza San Ulrich, is a delightful place to soak in the local ambiance.

During a recent journey through the region, I stumbled upon a small village called Sappada, which was not on my initial itinerary. The discovery was almost serendipitous, as I took a wrong turn while heading to a nearby town. What started as an unplanned detour turned into one of the most memorable parts of my trip.

Sappada, with its charming traditional houses and lush green meadows, exuded a serene atmosphere. I spent the day wandering through its peaceful streets, marveling at the intricate wooden façades of the houses, and enjoying a leisurely lunch at a local eatery. The villagers, with their warm hospitality, shared stories about the village's history and traditions, adding depth to my visit.

Recommendations

For those exploring these hidden gems, a visit to Canazei offers opportunities to explore nearby hiking trails and enjoy authentic mountain cuisine at local restaurants. The town's historical churches and traditional festivals provide further insight into its cultural heritage.

In Ortisei, make sure to visit the Museum Gherdëina, which showcases the region's rich history and woodcarving tradition. The local markets are perfect for finding unique souvenirs and experiencing the town's artisanal craftsmanship.

Sappada is ideal for outdoor enthusiasts, with its beautiful hiking trails and scenic landscapes. The local restaurants serve hearty, traditional dishes that highlight the region's culinary heritage.

Practical Information
Traveling to these hidden gems can be a delightful adventure in itself. Canazei and Ortisei are accessible by public transport, with regular bus services connecting them to larger cities. For Sappada, renting a car might be the most convenient option, as it allows for a more flexible exploration of the area.

Accommodation in these towns ranges from cozy guest houses to charming bed-and-breakfasts. Booking in advance is recommended, especially during peak seasons, to ensure a comfortable stay.

Exploring lesser-known towns and villages offers a chance to experience the region's true character and uncover hidden treasures that are often missed by conventional tourism. These hidden gems provide a unique perspective on local life and culture, enriching your journey with memorable encounters and discoveries. Embrace the opportunity to venture off the beaten path and appreciate the distinct charm that these lesser-known destinations have to offer.

CHAPTER 5

OUTDOOR ACTIVITIES

Hiking and Cycling Routes

Embark on an exhilarating summer adventure by exploring the stunning hiking and cycling opportunities that the region offers. This guide will help you navigate the diverse landscapes, from scenic trails to challenging routes, ensuring a memorable outdoor experience.

Hiking Routes

The region boasts a variety of hiking trails that cater to all levels of experience. For those new to hiking, the Val di Fassa Trail offers a relatively easy trek through picturesque meadows and gentle slopes. Spanning approximately 8 kilometers, this trail provides stunning views of the surrounding peaks and is perfect for a leisurely half-day hike. The terrain is predominantly flat with a few gentle inclines, making it accessible for families and beginners.

For more seasoned hikers, the Tre Cime di Lavaredo Circuit presents a more challenging adventure. This iconic 10-kilometer loop circles around the famed Tre Cime rock formations, offering breathtaking vistas of the Dolomites. The trail features varied terrain, including rocky paths and steep ascents, with a total elevation gain of around 600 meters. It usually takes about 4 to 5 hours to complete, and the views of the three towering peaks are well worth the effort.

Starting the Tre Cime di Lavaredo Circuit requires accessing the trailhead from the toll road at Misurina. Parking is available at the trailhead, but it's advisable to arrive early during peak season. Make sure to check weather conditions before setting out and bring essential gear, including sturdy hiking boots and layered clothing.

Cycling Routes

Cyclists can enjoy a range of routes, from tranquil scenic paths to rigorous mountain trails. The Sella Ronda Loop is a celebrated route among road cyclists. This 56-kilometer circuit traverses the Dolomite passes, offering panoramic views and a challenging ride with a total elevation gain of over 1,500 meters. It's a fantastic choice for experienced cyclists seeking a rewarding journey through stunning alpine scenery. The route starts and ends in Selva di Val Gardena, and it's recommended to rent a high-quality road bike to handle the demanding climbs and descents.

For mountain biking enthusiasts, the San Pellegrino Bike Park presents a network of trails that cater to various skill levels. The park includes a mix of cross-country and downhill routes, with scenic views and technical sections that challenge riders. The main loop covers approximately 20 kilometers and features several downhill segments and technical obstacles. Riders can access the park via the San Pellegrino Pass, where bike rentals and equipment are available.

Local hikers and cyclists recommend exploring the lesser-known Passo Giau area for both hiking and cycling. The trails here offer breathtaking, unobstructed views of the surrounding peaks and are often less crowded than the more popular routes. For a hidden gem, consider the Fanes-Sennes-Braies Natural Park, which offers a range of trails and cycling routes amidst pristine landscapes.

Seasonal considerations are important; summer months bring clear weather but can also attract crowds, so early morning starts are advisable to avoid the busiest times. Ensure you are prepared for sudden weather changes, as alpine conditions can vary.

Tips
When planning your adventures, consider staying in nearby towns like Selva di Val Gardena or Canazei, which offer convenient access to trailheads and cycling routes. Many local accommodations cater

specifically to outdoor enthusiasts, providing storage for equipment and local advice on the best routes.

Essential gear for hiking includes comfortable footwear, weather-appropriate clothing, a backpack with water, snacks, and a first aid kit. For cycling, a well-maintained bike, helmet, gloves, and hydration are crucial. If you're new to the area, local bike shops and outdoor stores can offer additional advice and equipment rentals.

The region's summer adventures offer diverse and exhilarating opportunities for both hikers and cyclists. Whether you're navigating the rugged trails of the Dolomites or cycling through scenic alpine passes, the outdoor experiences here promise to be unforgettable. Embrace the chance to explore the natural beauty of the area and create lasting memories through these adventurous activities.

Winter Sports: Skiing and Snowboarding

Explore the exhilarating world of winter sports with a detailed guide to skiing and snowboarding, showcasing the best options for an unforgettable experience. Whether you're a seasoned pro or new to the slopes, this guide will help you navigate the top destinations, understand the available options, and make the most of your winter adventure.

Overview of Winter Sports Destinations

The region is renowned for its premier ski resorts and snowboarding destinations, each offering unique features and breathtaking landscapes. Among the top resorts is Cortina d'Ampezzo, known for its stunning scenery and extensive ski terrain. Located in the heart of the Dolomites, Cortina offers a mix of challenging runs and gentle slopes, catering to all levels of skiers and snowboarders. Another notable destination is Val Gardena, part of the Dolomiti Superski area, which provides an extensive network of trails and excellent snow conditions throughout the season. Val Gardena's high-altitude location ensures reliable snowfall and well-maintained pistes.

The snow conditions in these regions are typically excellent, with abundant snowfall from December through April. Average temperatures range from mild to cold, depending on the altitude and time of year. Snow quality remains consistent, with powder conditions often found in the backcountry and well-groomed pistes in the resorts.

Skiing Options

For skiing enthusiasts, the region offers a variety of trails suited to different skill levels. In Cortina d'Ampezzo, the Forcella Rossa run stands out for advanced skiers, providing a thrilling descent with spectacular views of the surrounding peaks. Beginners will appreciate the gentle slopes at the Cinque Torr area, which offer a supportive environment for learning.

Lift systems at these resorts are designed for convenience and efficiency. Cortina features a mix of gondolas and chairlifts, including high-speed options that minimize wait times. Lift passes can be purchased for single days or multi-day access, with options for both ski-in/ski-out accommodations and regular lift access. In Val Gardena, the lift network is expansive, connecting to other resorts in the Dolomiti Superski area, allowing for extensive exploration of the region's trails.

Ski schools are readily available, offering lessons for all ages and skill levels. Cortina has several well-regarded ski schools, such as the Cortina Ski

School, which provides group and private lessons. Equipment rentals are also conveniently located, with shops offering a range of skis and accessories for every type of skier.

Snowboarding Options

Snowboarding enthusiasts will find ample opportunities at the region's resorts. Val Gardena boasts impressive snowboarding parks, including the Ursus Snowpark, which features a variety of terrain elements such as halfpipes, rail parks, and fun boxes. This park is known for hosting international competitions and offers features for both beginners and advanced riders.

For those interested in freestyle and backcountry snowboarding, Cortina offers exciting opportunities. The Faloria area is particularly popular for its diverse terrain and off-piste options, including guided backcountry tours that provide access to untouched powder and challenging terrain. Rental shops in Cortina, such as Cortina Ski Rental, provide high-quality snowboarding gear and equipment, while local instructors offer specialized lessons for freestyle and backcountry riding.

Recommendations for Beginners and Experts

For beginners, Val Gardena is highly recommended due to its extensive network of gentle slopes and highly rated ski schools. The resort's facilities and supportive environment make it an ideal location for those new to skiing or snowboarding.

Advanced skiers and snowboarders seeking a challenge should consider Cortina d'Ampezzo or La Villa, where rugged terrain and challenging runs await. The steep descents and off-piste options in these areas provide a rewarding experience for experienced winter sports enthusiasts.

Practical Information

When planning your winter sports trip, consider staying in accommodation that offers easy access to the slopes. Cortina and Val Gardena both provide a range of lodging options, from luxurious hotels to cozy chalets. Transportation to the resorts is typically straightforward, with options for car rentals, shuttle services, and public transportation.

Essential gear for skiing and snowboarding includes well-fitted boots, helmets, goggles, and weather-appropriate clothing. Dressing in layers and preparing for cold temperatures is crucial for comfort and safety. Local shops offer rentals and sales of all necessary equipment, ensuring that visitors are well-equipped for their adventures.

Local Insights

Local skiers and snowboarders recommend exploring some of the less crowded trails and parks to experience a more serene winter environment. Hidden spots like the Sella Ronda off-piste routes and lesser-known snowboarding parks provide unique opportunities away from the busier areas.

During the winter season, the region hosts various events, including snowboarding competitions and winter festivals. These events showcase local talent and provide an exciting addition to your winter sports itinerary.

The region's winter sports offerings provide a diverse range of experiences for skiing and snowboarding enthusiasts. From beginner-friendly slopes to challenging runs and impressive snowboarding parks, there is something for everyone. Embrace the opportunity to explore the region's stunning landscapes and enjoy a thrilling winter sports adventure.

Rock Climbing: Best Spots for All Levels

Discover the thrilling world of rock climbing with an in-depth guide to some of the best climbing spots, catering to climbers of all levels. Whether you're just starting out or seeking challenging ascents, this guide provides essential information to help you plan and enjoy your climbing adventures.

Overview of Climbing Destinations

In the region, several premier rock climbing destinations stand out for their unique features and climbing opportunities. Cortina d'Ampezzo is a renowned area, offering a mix of sport climbing and alpine routes set against stunning Dolomite peaks. The crags here are famous for their varied climbing styles and breathtaking scenery.

Another top destination is Arco, known for its sport climbing routes and vibrant climbing community. The area features a range of crags with well-bolted routes and a range of difficulty levels, making it a popular spot for climbers of all abilities. Finale Ligure, located on the Italian Riviera, is celebrated for its extensive sport climbing routes and beautiful coastal views, offering a unique blend of climbing and seaside relaxation.

Climbing Type and Style

Each climbing area is known for its distinct style and type of climbing. In Cortina d'Ampezzo, you'll find alpine climbing routes that offer high-altitude challenges and spectacular views. Arco excels in sport climbing with its well-maintained bolted routes, suitable for both beginners and advanced climbers. Finale Ligure combines sport climbing with bouldering, providing diverse climbing experiences in a stunning coastal setting.

Climbing Routes and Grades

For notable climbing routes, Cortina d'Ampezzo offers the"Via di Mezzo route, a classic alpine climb featuring varied terrain and incredible views. This route is known for its technical demands and is ideal for experienced climbers looking for a challenge.

InArco, the "Cengia di Campanile" route is popular among intermediate climbers for its moderate difficulty and well-protected sections. This route provides a good mix of climbing and scenic beauty.

Finale Ligure is home to the "Boulder Beach" area, which features a range of bouldering problems from beginner to advanced. This area is well-regarded for its diverse range of problems and stunning coastal backdrop.

Climbing grades in the region follow the French grading system, which ranges from 4a (easy) to 9b (extremely difficult). For example, a route graded 5c is considered moderately challenging, while a 7a route offers a more demanding climb.

Recommendations for Different Skill Levels

For beginners, Arco is an excellent choice due to its range of easier routes and well-established climbing schools. The area offers introductory programs and gentle climbs, providing a supportive environment for those new to climbing.

Intermediate and advanced climbers will find plenty of challenges in Cortina d'Ampezzo and Finale Ligure. Cortina offers alpine routes with varying difficulties, while Finale Ligure features challenging sport routes and bouldering problems that cater to more experienced climbers.

Practical Information

Accessing these climbing spots is generally straightforward.Cortina d'Ampezzois reachable by car or public transport from major cities, with ample parking available near the crags. Accommodations range from hotels to cozy lodges, catering to different budgets.

Arco is easily accessible by train or car, with several parking areas near the climbing crags. The town offers a range of accommodations, from campgrounds to upscale hotels.

Finale Ligure is well-connected by train and has parking available at the main climbing areas. The town offers various lodging options, including hostels and guesthouses.

Essential climbing gear includes harnesses, climbing shoes, helmets, and chalk. Local rental shops in each area offer equipment for all types of climbing. For alpine climbing inCortina, additional gear such as ropes, carabiners, and ice axes may be necessary.

Local climbers recommend visiting Arco during the spring and autumn months when the weather is ideal for climbing. In Cortina d'Ampezzo, early summer offers the best conditions for alpine routes, while Finale Ligure is most pleasant in the spring and autumn.

Safety and Environmental Tips
Safety is crucial in climbing, so always check your equipment before starting a climb and be aware of weather conditions. For alpine routes, ensure you are prepared for variable weather and carry the necessary gear.

Respecting the environment is important; practice Leave No Trace principles by packing out all trash and avoiding disturbance to wildlife. Follow local regulations and guidelines to help preserve climbing areas for future generations.

The region offers a wealth of climbing opportunities for all skill levels, from beginner-friendly routes to challenging ascents. Whether you're looking to scale the peaks of Cortina d'Ampezzo, enjoy sport climbing in Arco, or tackle bouldering problems in Finale Ligure, there's something for every climber. Explore these diverse climbing destinations and make the most of your climbing adventures.

Dolomite Trekking Routes: Trails for Every Adventurer

Embark on an unforgettable adventure through the Dolomites, a region renowned for its breathtaking landscapes and diverse trekking opportunities. This guide will lead you through some of the most captivating trekking routes in the Dolomites, offering detailed descriptions to help adventurers of all levels find their perfect trail.

Dolomite Trekking

The Dolomites, a mountain range in northeastern Italy, are celebrated for their dramatic peaks, lush valleys, and pristine alpine meadows. This UNESCO World Heritage site offers a wide range of trekking experiences, from leisurely strolls through verdant pastures to challenging ascents that reward climbers with panoramic views. The region's appeal lies in its diverse terrain, which caters to all levels of hikers and trekkers, making it a paradise for outdoor enthusiasts. The stunning geological formations and rich natural beauty promise an adventure that is both visually and physically rewarding.

Route Descriptions

One of the standout treks in the Dolomites is the Tre Cime di Lavaredo Loop. This iconic trail begins at the Auronzo Hut and circles the base of the Tre Cime peaks. The loop is approximately 10 kilometers long and typically takes 3 to 4 hours to complete. It is rated as moderate in difficulty, with well-marked paths and a few rocky sections. Trekkers are treated to spectacular views of the dramatic peaks and the surrounding valleys. The trail offers a relatively gentle ascent and descent, with an elevation gain of about 400 meters. The route is especially popular in the summer months when the wildflowers are in full bloom, adding vibrant colors to the rugged landscape.

Another notable route is the Sella Ronda Trek, a more challenging multi-day trek that traverses the Sella Massif. This route covers about 50 kilometers and usually takes 3 to 4 days to complete, depending on pace and stops. The trek is considered advanced due to its elevation changes, technical sections, and the need for strong physical fitness. The trail offers stunning views of the Sella Group and passes through several alpine huts where trekkers can rest and refuel. The Sella Ronda involves significant altitude changes, with an elevation gain and loss of approximately 2,500 meters. This trek is ideal for experienced hikers looking to immerse themselves in the dramatic landscapes of the Dolomites.

For beginners, the Lago di Braies Trail provides a scenic and accessible option. Starting at the Lago di Braies, this 4.5-kilometer loop trail takes about 1.5 to

2 hours to complete and is rated as easy. The path is mostly flat, following the shoreline of the lake, and offers breathtaking views of the turquoise water against the backdrop of the surrounding peaks. This trail is perfect for those new to trekking or those seeking a leisurely walk in an incredibly picturesque setting. The relatively easy terrain and short duration make it a popular choice for families and casual hikers.

Recommendations for Different Skill Levels

For beginners, the Lago di Braies Trail is highly recommended due to its ease of access and manageable difficulty. The gentle terrain and short distance make it an ideal introduction to trekking in the Dolomites. It provides an opportunity to experience the beauty of the region without the challenge of more strenuous hikes. The well-maintained path and breathtaking scenery ensure a rewarding experience for those who are new to trekking.

Intermediate trekkers may enjoy the Tre Cime di Lavaredo Loop. This trail offers a balance of moderate difficulty with rewarding views and varied terrain. The loop is manageable in a day, with well-marked paths that provide a sense of accomplishment without the more demanding requirements of longer or more technical routes. It is perfect for those who have some trekking experience and are looking to explore the Dolomites further.

For advanced trekkers, the Sella Ronda Trek presents a challenging and immersive experience. This multi-day trek demands strong physical fitness and technical skills, offering a deep dive into the Dolomites' rugged terrain. The extensive elevation changes and technical sections require careful preparation and planning. This trek is suited for experienced hikers seeking a comprehensive adventure through some of the most dramatic landscapes in the region.

Practical Information

Accessing these trails generally involves driving to the trailheads or using local public transportation. For the Tre Cime di Lavaredo Loop, parking is available at the Auronzo Hut, where the trail begins. Nearby accommodations range from mountain huts to hotels in surrounding towns like Cortina d'Ampezzo. The Sella Ronda Trek requires arrangements for overnight stays in alpine huts along the route, which should be booked in advance. The Lago di Braies Trail is accessible with ample parking and nearby facilities.

Essential gear for trekking in the Dolomites includes sturdy hiking boots, weather-appropriate clothing, and trekking poles. For more challenging routes like the Sella Ronda Trek, additional equipment such as a climbing helmet and harness may be necessary. Preparing for variable weather conditions is crucial, as temperatures can fluctuate and weather can change rapidly in the mountains.

Local Insights

Local guides recommend visiting the Dolomites in late summer or early autumn for the best trekking conditions. The weather is generally stable, and the trails are less crowded than in peak summer. Hidden gems include lesser-known trails such as the Fanes-Sennes-Braies Natural Park routes, which offer serene landscapes and fewer crowds. Personal stories from trekkers highlight the charm of staying in alpine huts and experiencing the hospitality of local hosts.

Safety and Environmental Tips

Safety is paramount when trekking in the Dolomites. Always check weather conditions before setting out and be prepared for sudden changes. Ensure that you are acclimated to the altitude, especially on high-altitude treks. Carry a map or GPS device, and let someone know your planned route and expected return time. Environmental responsibility is also important; follow Leave No Trace principles, respect wildlife, and stick to marked trails to help preserve the natural beauty of the region.

The Dolomites offer a diverse range of trekking opportunities, from beginner-friendly trails to challenging high-altitude routes. Whether you're seeking a leisurely walk around a picturesque lake or an advanced multi-day trek through rugged terrain, the Dolomites provide a stunning backdrop for memorable adventures. Explore these trails to experience the region's natural beauty and enjoy a rewarding trekking experience in one of the most spectacular mountain ranges in the world.

Mountain Biking Routes in the Dolomites

The Dolomites, with their rugged peaks and scenic valleys, are a premier destination for mountain biking enthusiasts. Whether you're seeking adrenaline-pumping descents or leisurely rides through picturesque landscapes, the region offers an array of routes that cater to all skill levels. Here's a guide to some of the top mountain biking trails.

1. Sella Ronda
One of the crown jewels of mountain biking in the Dolomites, the Sella Ronda is a thrilling loop that encircles the Sella Massif. Spanning approximately

60 kilometers, this route offers a blend of technical descents, challenging climbs, and breathtaking vistas. Starting from towns like Selva di Val Gardena, Arabba, or Corvara, the journey takes you through a variety of terrains, from rocky paths to lush alpine meadows.

To reach the Sella Ronda, head to these starting points via local transport or shuttles. The route is well-marked, but having a detailed map or GPS device is useful. For the best experience, aim to ride during sunrise or sunset, when the peaks are bathed in golden light, and the changing shadows create a dramatic backdrop.

2. Val di Fassa Bike Park

The Val di Fassa Bike Park is a haven for mountain bikers of all levels. Located in Canazei, this park offers a diverse range of trails, from beginner-friendly paths to advanced technical descents. The bike park is easily accessible from Canazei via local cable cars or by biking up from the town.

If you're coming from larger towns like Bolzano, you can take a train and then a bus to Canazei. Once there, you'll find well-maintained trails that showcase the beauty of the Val di Fassa valley. Whether you're looking for flowy singletracks or challenging sections with jumps and berms, the park has something for everyone. Early morning rides offer a peaceful atmosphere and beautiful light, perfect for capturing the valley's serene beauty.

3. Alta Badia Trails

In the Alta Badia region, a network of trails awaits riders eager to explore the picturesque valley. Starting from Corvara or La Villa, you can access a variety of trails that meander through charming alpine scenery. These trails are suitable for beginners and intermediate riders, offering a mix of smooth paths and more technical sections.

To get to Alta Badia, use local buses or drive to these towns, where you'll find ample parking and bike rental options. The trails here are well-marked, and local tourist offices provide detailed maps. For a memorable ride, plan your journey during the late afternoon when the setting sun casts a warm glow over the landscape, highlighting the stunning views.

4. Cortina d'Ampezzo Trails

Cortina d'Ampezzo is a vibrant hub for mountain biking, featuring trails that cater to various skill levels. From easy rides through scenic valleys to challenging alpine routes, the area offers a range of options. Start your adventure from Cortina, which is well-connected by train and bus from major cities.

Local bike rental shops and shuttle services are available to help you reach the trails. The diverse terrain includes singletracks, technical descents, and panoramic climbs. For the most striking photographs and an exhilarating ride, aim for early morning or late afternoon, when the light enhances the natural beauty of the peaks and valleys.

5. Alpe di Siusi (Seiser Alm)

Alpe di Siusi, or Seiser Alm, is a must-visit for mountain bikers seeking breathtaking views and varied terrain. Accessible from Ortisei via a scenic cable car ride, this plateau offers a network of trails that traverse stunning meadows and provide panoramic mountain vistas.

Ortisei is reachable by train and bus from Bolzano, and once you arrive, you can take the cable car up to the Alpe di Siusi. The trails here cater to beginners and intermediate riders, featuring well-marked routes through picturesque alpine scenery. Sunrise or sunset rides provide the best lighting for capturing the sweeping views and the beautiful interplay of shadows and light across the meadows.

Tips for Mountain Biking in the Dolomites

- Preparation: Ensure your bike is in good condition before heading out. Local bike shops offer repairs and rentals if needed.

- Maps and Navigation: Carry GPS device. Trails are well-marked, but a GPS map ensures you stay on track.

- Weather: Be prepared for changing weather conditions. The weather in the mountains can shift quickly, so bring appropriate clothing and gear.
- Safety: Always wear a helmet and protective gear. Some trails can be challenging, so make sure you're comfortable with the level of difficulty.

These routes highlight the diverse beauty of the Dolomites, offering unforgettable experiences for mountain biking enthusiasts. Whether you're tackling the famous Sella Ronda loop or enjoying the scenic trails of Alpe di Siusi, the Dolomites provide an exhilarating and memorable adventure for riders of all skill levels.

CHAPTER 6
EXPERIENCING THE DOLOMITES

Overview of Cultural Institutions

The Dolomites are not only a paradise for nature lovers but also a treasure trove of cultural and historical riches. The region boasts numerous cultural institutions, including museums, galleries, historical landmarks, theaters, and cultural centers. These institutions play a crucial role in preserving and celebrating the local heritage, arts, and traditions. Among the most notable are the South Tyrol Museum of Archaeology in Bolzano, the Ladin Museum in San Martin de Tor, and the Messner Mountain Museum. Each offers unique exhibits, architectural features, and programs that make them distinct and essential stops for any visitor interested in the cultural fabric of the Dolomites.

The cultural institutions in the Dolomites are deeply intertwined with the region's rich history and heritage. The South Tyrol Museum of Archaeology, for instance, is renowned for housing Ötzi the Iceman, a well-preserved natural mummy from about 3300 BCE, which offers profound insights into prehistoric life in the Alps. The Ladin Museum, on the other hand, focuses on the Ladin culture, a unique ethnic group in the Dolomites with a distinct language and traditions. The Messner Mountain Museum, founded by the legendary mountaineer Reinhold Messner, celebrates the history and culture of mountaineering, providing a deep dive into the human relationship with the mountains. These institutions not only safeguard the region's past but also educate and inspire future generations.

The South Tyrol Museum of Archaeology in Bolzano is a must-visit for history enthusiasts. Its star attraction, Ötzi the Iceman, is complemented by exhibits that explore the life and times of this ancient inhabitant. The museum also features rotating exhibits on various archaeological topics, offering fresh insights on each visit. Architecturally, the building is a blend of modern and traditional styles, with spacious, well-lit galleries that enhance the display of artifacts.

The Ladin Museum in San Martin de Tor offers an intimate look at the Ladin people's culture and history. Exhibits include traditional clothing, tools, and artworks that depict the daily life and customs of the Ladin people. The museum is housed in a beautifully restored manor, which itself is a testament to the architectural heritage of the region.

Must-Visit Historical Sites and Museums in the Dolomites

The Dolomites are not only renowned for their stunning natural beauty but also for their rich cultural and historical heritage. Exploring the region's historical sites and museums offers a fascinating glimpse into the past, revealing how the Dolomites have evolved through millennia. From ancient artifacts and medieval fortresses to wartime bunkers and mining heritage, these sites provide a deep and engaging understanding of the region's diverse history. Here's a guide to some of the must-visit historical sites and museums in the Dolomites:

1. Messner Mountain Museum – Firmian

Situated in a striking castle overlooking Bolzano, the Messner Mountain Museum – Firmian offers a unique exploration of mountain cultures and the history of alpine climbing.

- Location and Directions: The museum is located at Schloss Sigmundskron (Firmian Castle) in Bolzano. To reach it, take the A22 highway to Bolzano and follow signs for Firmian Castle. The castle is about a 15-minute drive from the city center and is also accessible by a 30-minute walk or local bus service.

The Messner Mountain Museum – Firmian is part of a series of museums founded by the legendary climber Reinhold Messner. The museum is housed in a medieval castle, and its exhibits focus on the culture and history of mountain communities around the world. The museum's collection includes climbing equipment, historical artifacts, and art that reflects the mountain experience. One highlight is the interactive display on Messner's own climbing expeditions, offering a personal perspective on the challenges and triumphs of alpine climbing. The castle itself, with its panoramic views of the surrounding valley and mountains, provides a dramatic backdrop to the exhibits.

2. Geological Museum of the Dolomites
Located in the heart of the Dolomites, this museum in the town of Cortina d'Ampezzo offers an in-depth look at the natural and human history of the region.

- Location and Directions: The museum is situated in Cortina d'Ampezzo, a well-known resort town. To get there, drive along the SR48 from the A22 highway, following signs to Cortina. The museum is centrally located near the town's main attractions.

The Dolomites Museum provides a comprehensive overview of the region's geological and human history. The exhibits cover the formation of the Dolomites, including detailed models and interactive displays explaining the unique geology of the area. You'll also find sections dedicated to the local flora and fauna, showcasing the biodiversity of the Dolomites. The museum includes historical artifacts that illustrate the traditional life of the local mountain communities, including tools, clothing, and everyday items. The museum's focus on both natural history and cultural heritage offers a well-rounded understanding of the Dolomites.

3. The Great War Museum at Marmolada

The Museum of the Great War at Marmolada is located on the highest peak in the Dolomites and provides a poignant look at the region's role in World War I.

- Location and Directions: The museum is situated at Punta Serauta on the Marmolada massif. To reach it, take the cable car from Malga Ciapela to the summit. The museum is located within the historical military fortifications on the peak.

The Museum of the Great War at Marmolada offers a powerful insight into the wartime history of the Dolomites. The exhibits are housed in a restored military fort and include original wartime artifacts, photographs, and personal stories from soldiers. The museum provides a detailed account of the strategic significance of Marmolada during the war, with displays on the harsh conditions faced by soldiers. Walking through the old trenches and bunkers, visitors gain a tangible sense of the wartime experience. The breathtaking views from the summit, combined with the historical context, make this a memorable visit.

4. The South Tyrol Museum of Archaeology

Although just outside the Dolomites, this museum in Bolzano is essential for understanding the prehistoric and early historical context of the region.

- Location and Directions: The museum is located in Bolzano, South Tyrol. To get there, drive via the A22 highway to Bolzano, then follow signs to the city center. The museum is centrally located near Bolzano's historic district.

The South Tyrol Museum of Archaeology is renowned for housing the famous Ötzi the Iceman, a naturally mummified man from the Copper Age. The museum offers a fascinating glimpse into prehistoric life with its collection of artifacts, including Ötzi's clothing, tools, and personal items. Detailed exhibits explain the scientific analysis of Ötzi and what it reveals about his life and environment. The museum also features interactive displays and reconstructions that bring the prehistoric world to life. Visiting this museum provides a deeper understanding of the ancient cultures that once inhabited the region.

5. Museo delle Minere di Predazzo

The Museo delle Minere di Predazzo, located in Predazzo, offers insights into the region's mining history and its impact on local development.

- Location and Directions: The museum is situated in Predazzo, a town in the Val di Fiemme. To get there, drive from Cavalese via SS48, following signs to Predazzo. The museum is centrally located in town.

Museo delle Minere di Predazzo highlights the significance of mining in the Dolomites. Exhibits cover the extraction of various minerals, including iron and zinc, and feature displays on mining technology and daily life in the mines. Visitors can explore a reconstructed mine shaft and see historical mining equipment. The museum also provides a historical narrative on the evolution of mining practices and their effects on the local community. The engaging exhibits and interactive elements make it a fascinating visit for those interested in industrial history.

6. Ladin Museum (Museo Ladin)

Location and Directions: The Ladin Museum is located in San Martin de Tor, a village in the Val Badia. To reach it, drive along the SR48 from Brunico, following signs to San Martin de Tor. The museum is situated in the village center, easily accessible by car.

The Ladin Museum provides a deep dive into the Ladin culture and heritage of the Dolomites. The museum's exhibits include traditional Ladin artifacts, historical documents, and displays on the region's unique language and customs. Visitors can explore the Ladin way of life through reconstructed settings that showcase traditional farming practices, crafts, and festivals. The museum offers interactive displays and personal stories that highlight the significance of Ladin traditions. A visit here helps you appreciate the rich cultural tapestry of the Dolomites and the efforts to preserve Ladin heritage

These historical sites and museums provide a rich tapestry of the Dolomites' past, from ancient artifacts and medieval art to wartime history and industrial heritage. Each location offers a unique perspective, enhancing your understanding and appreciation of this remarkable region.

Practical Information

The South Tyrol Museum of Archaeology operates from 10 AM to 6 PM daily, with extended hours until 8 PM on Thursdays. Admission fees are €9 for adults, with discounts available for students, seniors, and children. The museum also offers free admission on the first Sunday of each month. Special programs include guided tours and educational workshops, often held during the summer months.

The Ladin Museum is open from 10 AM to 5 PM, Tuesday through Sunday. Admission is €7, with discounts for groups, students, and seniors. The museum hosts cultural events and temporary exhibitions, which provide deeper insights into the Ladin way of life. Workshops on traditional crafts and language courses are also available.

The Messner Mountain Museum's Corones branch is open from 10 AM to 5 PM daily, from late May to early November. Admission is €10, with reduced rates for families and groups. Special events include lectures by Reinhold Messner and film screenings on mountaineering. The museum also offers themed tours that delve into specific aspects of mountain culture and history.

Visitor Tips
For the best experience at the South Tyrol Museum of Archaeology, visit early in the morning or late in the afternoon to avoid crowds. The museum is located in Bolzano, which has numerous dining options ranging from traditional South Tyrolean cuisine to modern eateries. Accessibility features include ramps and elevators, ensuring a comfortable visit for all guests.

When visiting the Ladin Museum, plan to spend a few hours exploring the exhibits and the surrounding area. San Martin de Tor has charming local cafes where you can enjoy traditional Ladin dishes. The museum is wheelchair accessible, and guided tours are available for visitors with visual or hearing impairments.

To fully enjoy the Messner Mountain Museum Corones, allocate a full day for your visit. The journey to the mountaintop location is part of the experience, with cable car rides offering stunning views. The museum has a cafe with panoramic views, perfect for a break during your visit. Dress warmly, even in summer, as temperatures can be cooler at higher altitudes.

Local Insights

Local experts suggest exploring lesser-known cultural sites such as the Museum Ladin Ursus Ladinicus in San Cassiano, which focuses on the prehistoric cave bear and its significance to the region. Another hidden gem is the Ethnographic Museum in Dietenheim, which offers a deep dive into rural life in the Dolomites through its extensive collection of artifacts and reconstructed historical buildings. These sites provide unique insights and are often less crowded than the more famous institutions.

The cultural institutions of the Dolomites offer a window into the rich history and heritage of the region. From the ancient past revealed at the South Tyrol Museum of Archaeology to the living traditions showcased at the Ladin Museum, and the adventurous spirit celebrated at the Messner Mountain Museum, these sites provide invaluable insights into the area's cultural fabric. Exploring these museums and historical sites allows visitors to gain a deeper understanding and appreciation of the Dolomites' unique cultural landscape. Whether you are a history buff, an art lover, or an adventure seeker, the cultural institutions of the Dolomites offer something for everyone, making them essential stops on any itinerary.

Traditional Festivals

The Dolomites region is rich in cultural traditions, with festivals that celebrate its heritage and community spirit. Key festivals include the South Tyrolean Christmas Markets, the Ladin Carnival, and the Transhumance Festival. The South Tyrolean Christmas Markets, held from late November to early January in various towns such as Bolzano, Merano, and Bressanone, are renowned for their festive charm and unique Alpine atmosphere. The Ladin Carnival, celebrated in February across Laden-speaking valleys, is known for its vibrant parades and traditional masks. The Transhumance Festival, held in September in valleys like Val di Funes, marks the seasonal movement of livestock with processions and folkloric events. These festivals are not just events but deep-rooted traditions that showcase the region's cultural vibrancy.

Each festival in the Dolomites carries significant historical and cultural importance. The South Tyrolean Christmas Markets are a testament to the region's blend of Germanic and Italian traditions, featuring handcrafted ornaments, local delicacies, and festive music that reflect the area's multicultural heritage. The Ladin Carnival is deeply rooted in the Ladin culture, with traditions dating back centuries. The intricate masks worn during the parades symbolize ancient folklore and community identity.

The Transhumance Festival celebrates an age-old pastoral tradition, highlighting the vital role of agriculture and livestock in the region's history. These festivals not only preserve ancient customs but also foster a sense of community and continuity, connecting generations through shared cultural practices.

The South Tyrolean Christmas Markets transform the towns into winter wonderlands. Streets are adorned with twinkling lights, and the air is filled with the scent of spiced mulled wine and gingerbread. Wooden stalls sell handmade crafts, local foods, and festive decorations, while choirs and musicians perform carols, creating a joyful atmosphere. The highlight is the giant Christmas tree in Bolzano's main square, a dazzling spectacle that draws visitors from around the world.

The Ladin Carnival is a riot of color and sound. Participants don elaborate costumes and masks, many handcrafted with intricate details, representing various characters from local legends. Parades wind through villages, accompanied by traditional music and dance. The carnival culminates in the burning of the Carnival King, a symbolic act meant to chase away winter and herald the arrival of spring. The festival is marked by communal feasts, where traditional dishes like barley soup and krapfen (fried pastries) are enjoyed.

The Transhumance Festival is a picturesque celebration of pastoral life. Herds of cows, adorned with floral wreaths and bells, are led through villages in a grand procession. Shepherds and farmers, dressed in traditional attire, follow, showcasing their skills and the strong bond between humans and animals. The festival includes folk dances, music, and craft demonstrations, providing a glimpse into rural traditions. The highlight is the blessing of the animals, a ritual that underscores the community's respect for livestock and nature.

Attending the South Tyrolean Christmas Market in Bolzano was a magical experience. Drawn by the promise of festive cheer, I arrived just as twilight was settling in. The sight of the illuminated market, with its myriad stalls and the towering Christmas tree, was breathtaking. I meandered through the stalls, savoring the flavors of roasted chestnuts and warming up with a cup of mulled wine. A particularly memorable moment was watching a group of children perform traditional carols, their voices blending harmoniously with the crisp winter air. Engaging with local artisans, I learned about the craftsmanship behind the intricate wooden toys and ornaments. This experience deepened my appreciation for the region's traditions and the communal effort that goes into keeping them alive.

Practical Information

To fully enjoy these festivals, planning is essential. The South Tyrolean Christmas Markets run from late November to early January, with Bolzano, Merano, and Bressanone being key locations. Book accommodations well in advance, as these towns become quite popular during the festive season. Dress warmly and bring a camera to capture the magical moments.

The Ladin Carnival takes place in February, primarily in the Ladin-speaking valleys. Check local schedules for specific dates and locations of parades. Comfortable shoes are recommended for walking through the villages and participating in the festivities.

The Transhumance Festival is held in September, with Val di Funes being a notable venue. Early arrival is advisable to secure a good spot for viewing the procession. Bring a hat and sunscreen, as the weather can be sunny.

Visitor Tips

For the Christmas Markets, visiting on weekdays can help avoid the weekend crowds. Sample local specialties such as Zelten (fruitcake) and Speck (cured ham). In Bolzano, the Waltherplatz is the heart of the market, offering the best photo opportunities.

During the Ladin Carnival, try to join a guided tour to understand the significance of the masks and costumes. Local inns often serve special carnival menus, providing a chance to taste authentic Ladin cuisine. At the Transhumance Festival, interact with the shepherds to learn about their way of life. The village of Santa Maddalena in Val di Funes offers stunning backdrops for photos, with the Dolomites in the distance.

Locals suggest exploring the smaller, less touristy Christmas markets in towns like Vipiteno and Brunico, which offer a more intimate experience. The Carnival in lesser-known villages like Campill can provide a more authentic glimpse into Ladin traditions.

For the Transhumance Festival, attending the early morning preparations gives a deeper insight into the shepherds' rituals and the care they take in adorning their animals. Engaging with the locals can also lead to discovering hidden gems, like secret viewing spots or local delicacies not found in guidebooks.

Experiencing the traditional festivals of the Dolomites offers a unique window into the region's rich cultural heritage. These celebrations, with their vibrant displays of local traditions, music, and cuisine, provide a deep connection to the community and its history. By immersing yourself in these festivals, you gain a profound appreciation for the Dolomites' cultural tapestry, making your visit to this stunning region all the more memorable. Whether it's the festive spirit of the Christmas markets, the vibrant colors of the Ladin Carnival, or the pastoral charm of the Transhumance Festival, each event offers a unique and enriching experience that showcases the enduring spirit and traditions of the Dolomites.

Dining: Must- Try Local Restaurants

The Dolomites offer a diverse and vibrant dining scene that reflects its rich cultural heritage. One must-try restaurant is Ristorante St. Hubertus in San Cassiano, this restaurant provides a fine dining experience in a cozy, rustic setting. Another notable spot is Rifugio Fodara Vedla, a farm-to-table restaurant located in the heart of the Fanes-Sennes-Braies Natural Park. It offers a cozy, mountain lodge atmosphere with stunning views and dishes crafted from locally sourced ingredients. For a more casual experience, Osteria Acquarol in Appiano is a hidden gem offering a modern twist on South Tyrolean classics, where diners can enjoy a relaxed, family-friendly setting. In Bolzano, Ristorante Vögele stands out with its historical charm and diverse menu that showcases local flavors with a contemporary flair.

Restaurant Details

Ristorante St. Hubertus in San Cassiano offers an intimate and romantic atmosphere with wooden interiors and elegant decor. The price range is upscale, with appetizers averaging around €30, main courses €55, and desserts €20. Signature dishes include the venison with juniper and the innovative hay-smoked trout.

Rifugio Fodara Vedla exudes a rustic, family-friendly ambiance, with pricing that is moderate: appetizers around €15, main courses €25, and desserts €10. Their signature dishes include polenta with local mushrooms and homemade dumplings.

Osteria Acquarol in Appiano has a casual, welcoming atmosphere, with prices that are accessible: appetizers around €10, main courses €20, and desserts €8. Not to be missed are their house-made ravioli and the slow-cooked lamb.

Ristorante Vögele in Bolzano offers a blend of historical and modern vibes, with a moderate price range: appetizers around €12, main courses €22, and desserts €9. Signature dishes include their traditional South Tyrolean knödel and the apple strudel.

Nightlife Scene

The Dolomites' nightlife is as diverse as its dining options, offering something for everyone. In Bolzano, Hopfen & Co. is a popular bar known for its lively atmosphere and extensive selection of local and international beers. The pub also offers traditional pub fare and occasionally hosts live music. Another favorite is Laurin Bar, located in the historic Parkhotel Laurin. This elegant bar offers a sophisticated setting with a range of craft cocktails and a beautiful garden area for outdoor seating. For live music enthusiasts, Club Moritzino in Corvara is a must-visit. This venue offers live performances ranging from jazz to contemporary hits, set against the stunning backdrop of the Dolomites. The bar's alpine chic interior and extensive drink menu make it a perfect spot for an evening out. For those looking to dance the night away,Hexen Klub in Ortisei is a popular nightclub featuring high-energy vibes, electronic music, and guest DJs from across Europe. The club's sleek, modern design and vibrant atmosphere attract both locals and tourists.

Dining out in the Dolomites often means embracing local customs and traditions. Meals are typically leisurely affairs, especially dinner, which is usually enjoyed over several courses. It's common to start with an aperitif, such as a glass of local wine or a spritz, and end with a digestif like grappa. In many family-run eateries, you'll find dishes passed down through generations, showcasing the region's culinary heritage. Nightlife in the Dolomites also reflects local culture, with a strong emphasis on community and hospitality. Bars and pubs often serve as social hubs where locals gather to unwind and socialize. Understanding these nuances can enhance your dining and nightlife experiences, providing deeper insights into the region's way of life.

Hidden Gems

Among the hidden gems in the Dolomites is Manna Del Brenta, a secluded bistro in San Martino di Castrozza. This family-run establishment offers an intimate dining experience with a focus on seasonal, locally sourced ingredients. The warm, welcoming atmosphere makes it a perfect spot for a cozy dinner. Another lesser-known spot is Bar Licino in Cortina d'Ampezzo, a tucked-away speakeasy known for its craft cocktails and vintage decor. The bar's low-key vibe and expert mixologists create a unique and memorable night out. For a more rustic experience, Rifugio Averau located high in the mountains, provides breathtaking views and hearty local fare. Accessible only by a scenic hike or cable car, this hidden gem offers an authentic taste of mountain life.

To fully enjoy the nightlife in the Dolomites safely, it's essential to plan your transportation in advance. Many towns have limited public transport options late at night, so consider booking a taxi or arranging a designated driver. Local laws regarding alcohol consumption are similar to other parts of Italy, with a legal drinking age of 18. Be mindful of areas that might be less populated late at night, especially in more remote villages, and stick to well-lit and busy streets. It's also advisable to carry some cash, as not all establishments accept credit cards. Lastly, always drink responsibly and be aware of your surroundings to ensure a safe and enjoyable night out.

The dining and nightlife scene in the Dolomites is a vibrant tapestry of experiences, offering everything from high-end culinary delights to cozy, family-run eateries, and lively bars to sophisticated nightclubs. The region's cultural heritage is richly reflected in its food and social venues, providing visitors with a unique and immersive experience. Whether you're savoring a gourmet meal in a Michelin-starred restaurant, enjoying a craft cocktail in a hidden speakeasy, or dancing the night away in a bustling nightclub, the Dolomites' diverse offerings ensure that every visitor can find something to enjoy. Embrace the local customs, explore the hidden gems, and immerse yourself in the vibrant dining and nightlife scene to fully experience the heart and soul of the Dolomites.

Local Cuisine

The Dolomites offer a rich tapestry of culinary delights that reflect the region's Alpine roots and Italian influences. From hearty mountain fare to delicate pastries, the local cuisine provides a flavorful introduction to the region's culture and traditions.

1. Speck and Cheese Platters

A staple of Dolomite cuisine, speck is a dry-cured ham that is seasoned with a blend of spices and aged to develop a distinctive smoky flavor. It is often enjoyed as part of a charcuterie platter, accompanied by a selection of local cheeses, such as Graukäse. Graukäse is a semi-hard cheese with a tangy, slightly crumbly texture that complements the rich, savory taste of the speck. The platter is typically served with fresh crusty bread, pickles, and sometimes mustard, creating a well-rounded appetizer that showcases the region's traditional flavors.

2. Canederli (Dumplings)

Canederli are traditional dumplings made from stale bread, milk, eggs, and sometimes mixed with ingredients such as speck or cheese. These dumplings are either boiled and served in a savory broth or pan-fried and topped with melted butter and herbs. The texture of canederli is hearty and comforting, making them a popular choice in the

Dolomites, especially during colder months. The dumplings absorb the flavors of their accompanying broth or sauce, creating a satisfying and flavorful dish. During a visit to Val Gardena, I enjoyed canederli in a rustic alpine restaurant. The dumplings were served in a rich, aromatic broth with a sprinkle of fresh parsley.

3. Polenta

Polenta is a versatile dish made from cornmeal, and it holds a special place in Dolomite cuisine. It can be served soft, like a creamy porridge, or allowed to set and then grilled or fried to form a crispy crust. Polenta is commonly paired with rich meat dishes, stews, or hearty sauces. Its mild, slightly sweet flavor acts as a perfect base for more robust flavors, making it a versatile accompaniment to a variety of Dolomite specialties.

4. Strudel

Strudel is a popular dessert in the Dolomites, consisting of a flaky pastry filled with a mixture of spiced apples, raisins, and cinnamon. The pastry is typically rolled thin and filled with the apple mixture before being baked to a golden brown. Once out of the oven, the strudel is often dusted with powdered sugar and served warm. The combination of the crisp pastry and the tender, spiced apple filling makes for a delightful and comforting dessert.

5. Local Wines and Grappa

The Dolomites are also known for their local wines and grappa. Gewürztraminer and Lagrein are two notable wines from the region. Gewürztraminer is a white wine with aromatic floral notes and a hint of spice, while Lagrein is a red wine with a deep, rich flavor and smooth finish. Grappa, a pomace brandy, is a traditional Italian digestif made from the remnants of winemaking. It is typically enjoyed after a meal for its warming, slightly fruity qualities.

The local cuisine of the Dolomites offers a rich array of flavors and dishes that capture the essence of the region. Each dish, from the hearty canederli to the delicate strudel, reflects the culinary heritage of this mountainous region. The food is characterized by its use of local ingredients and traditional cooking methods, providing a true taste of the Dolomites' culture and landscape.

Souvenirs and Shopping in the Dolomites

Shopping in the Dolomites offers a delightful blend of unique local products, traditional crafts, and memorable souvenirs that reflect the rich cultural heritage and natural beauty of the region. From artisanal goods to gourmet treats, there's something special for every traveler to take home.

Handcrafted Wood Items

One of the most traditional and cherished souvenirs from the Dolomites is handcrafted wooden items. The region is renowned for its skilled woodworkers who create everything from intricate carvings to functional kitchenware. Val Gardena, in particular, is famous for its wood carving tradition. Visitors can find beautifully carved religious figures, nativity scenes, and decorative items in local shops. A visit to a woodcarving workshop can offer a fascinating glimpse into this ancient craft, allowing you to see artisans at work and purchase unique pieces directly from the source. These handcrafted items make for a meaningful and authentic souvenir that captures the essence of the Dolomites' artistic heritage.

Loden Wool Products

Loden wool, known for its durability and warmth, is a signature product of the Dolomites. This traditional fabric is made from sheep's wool that is felted to create a dense, water-resistant material. Loden wool is used to craft a variety of clothing items, including jackets, capes, hats, and scarves. Shopping for Loden wool products in the Dolomites provides an opportunity to purchase high-quality, long-lasting garments that are both functional and stylish. Bolzano is a great place to find specialty shops offering a wide range of Loden products. These items not only serve as practical souvenirs but also as a piece of the region's cultural heritage.

Artisanal Food and Drink

The culinary delights of the Dolomites make for excellent souvenirs. Local cheeses, such as Pustertaler Bergkäse and Graukäse, offer a taste of the region's rich dairy tradition. These cheeses are often available at local markets and specialty shops. For those with a sweet tooth, Südtiroler Zelten, a traditional fruit bread made with nuts and dried fruits, is a must-try. Local honey, jams, and herbal teas are also popular choices that capture the flavors of the region. Don't forget to explore local wines from the South Tyrol wine region, such as Gewürztraminer and Lagrein. Many wineries offer tours and tastings, providing an opportunity to learn about the winemaking process and purchase bottles directly from the source.

Traditional Alpine Clothing

Traditional Alpine clothing, such as dirndls for women and lederhosen for men, are iconic symbols of the Dolomites' cultural heritage. These garments are often worn during local festivals and celebrations. Purchasing a dirndl or lederhosen from the Dolomites not only provides a unique and memorable souvenir but also supports the preservation of traditional dress. Shops in towns like Ortisei and Cortina d'Ampezzo offer a range of styles, from elaborate festival attire to more casual everyday wear. Wearing these traditional clothes allows you to fully immerse yourself in the local culture and brings a piece of the Dolomites' vibrant traditions back home.

Local Artwork and Photography

The stunning landscapes of the Dolomites have inspired countless artists and photographers. Local galleries and studios often feature works that capture the beauty of the mountains, valleys, and villages. Purchasing a piece of local artwork or a photograph provides a lasting reminder of your visit and supports the region's artistic community. Many artists are happy to share the stories behind their work, adding a personal touch to your souvenir.

Whether it's a watercolor painting of a mountain scene or a black-and-white photograph of a historic village, these pieces of art make for beautiful and meaningful keepsakes.

Practical Shopping Tips

When shopping for souvenirs in the Dolomites, it's helpful to keep a few practical tips in mind. Many towns have weekly markets where you can find a variety of local products and interact directly with the producers. These markets are great places to discover unique items and learn more about the region's traditions. It's also advisable to carry some cash, as smaller shops and market stalls may not accept credit cards. Take the time to explore local shops and talk to the owners or artisans; they often have fascinating stories to share about their crafts and products. Additionally, consider the practicality of transporting your souvenirs, especially if purchasing larger items like wooden carvings or bottles of wine.

Cultural Insights

Understanding the cultural significance of your souvenirs can greatly enrich your shopping experience. Many of the traditional crafts and products in the Dolomites are rooted in centuries-old traditions and reflect the region's unique blend of Italian and Austrian influences. For example, the intricate designs of wood carvings often incorporate religious and folkloric themes, highlighting the region's deep-rooted cultural beliefs. Similarly, Loden wool products connect to the region's agricultural history and the practical needs of mountain life. By learning about the origins and significance of these items, you gain a deeper appreciation for the craftsmanship and cultural heritage they represent.

While popular towns like Bolzano, Cortina d'Ampezzo, and Ortisei offer a wide range of shopping opportunities, some of the best finds can be discovered off the beaten path. Exploring smaller villages and rural areas can lead to the discovery of hidden gems, such as family-run workshops and local markets that offer unique products not found in larger tourist areas. These hidden gems often provide a more intimate and authentic shopping experience, allowing you to connect with local artisans and gain insight into their way of life. Keep an eye out for local festivals and events, where you can find an array of traditional crafts and regional specialties.

Shopping in the Dolomites offers a rich and rewarding experience, allowing travelers to take home a piece of the region's unique cultural heritage.

CHAPTER 7
ITINERARY

Weekend Getaway (2-3 Days)

Day 1: Arrival and Exploration of Bolzano

Arrive in Bolzano, the gateway to the Dolomites, and check into a centrally located hotel like Parkhotel Laurin, known for its elegant ambiance and convenient location. Spend your morning exploring Bolzano's historic center, starting with a visit to Piazza Walther, the city's main square. Enjoy a coffee at a local café while taking in the vibrant atmosphere. Next, head to the South Tyrol Museum of Archaeology to see the famous Ötzi the Iceman. For lunch, try a traditional South Tyrolean dish at Hopfen & Co., a popular local eatery. In the afternoon, take the Renon cable car for breathtaking views of the surrounding mountains and a leisurely hike on the Renon Plateau. End your day with dinner at Restaurant Vögele, which offers a mix of traditional and modern cuisine in a historical setting.

Day 2: Discovering Val Gardena

Start your day early with a drive to Val Gardena, one of the most picturesque valleys in the Dolomites.

Check into Hotel Alpenroyal Grand Hotel Gourmet & Spa in Selva di Val Gardena, a luxurious choice for accommodation. Begin your exploration with a visit to the charming village of Ortisei. Stroll through its pedestrian-friendly center, admiring the colorful buildings and artisan shops. For lunch, try the local specialties at Tubladel, known for its cozy atmosphere and delicious regional cuisine. In the afternoon, take the Seceda cable car up to the Seceda mountain, offering stunning panoramic views and numerous hiking trails. Return to Selva di Val Gardena for a relaxing evening, enjoying a gourmet dinner at the hotel's restaurant, which features a menu inspired by local and Mediterranean flavors.

Day 3: Hiking and Departure

On your final day, embark on a morning hike to the famous Alpe di Siusi, the largest high-altitude Alpine meadow in Europe. The rolling meadows, dotted with traditional huts, provide an idyllic setting for a leisurely hike or a more challenging trek, depending on your preference. After a refreshing morning, have lunch at Gostner Schwaige, a charming mountain hut renowned for its fresh, farm-to-table dishes. After lunch, return to Bolzano, making time for a quick visit to the local markets to pick up some regional specialties like speck or alpine cheeses before heading to the airport or train station for your departure.

Midweek Escape (4-5 Days)

Day 1: Arrival in Bolzano

Arrive in Bolzano and settle into your accommodation at the historic Parkhotel Laurin. Spend your first day exploring the city's cultural landmarks, including the South Tyrol Museum of Archaeology and the Bolzano Cathedral. Enjoy a leisurely lunch at Hopfen & Co., and in the afternoon, visit the Renon Plateau via the Renon cable car. Conclude your day with dinner at Restaurant Vögele, savoring the mix of traditional and contemporary dishes.

Day 2: Journey to Val Gardena

Head to Val Gardena and check into Hotel Alpenroyal Grand Hotel Gourmet & Spa. Start your exploration in Ortisei, visiting its vibrant center and artisan shops. Have lunch at Tubladel, then take the Seceda cable car for an afternoon of breathtaking views and hiking. Return to your hotel for a relaxing evening and a gourmet dinner.

Day 3: Adventure in Alpe di Siusi

Spend the day at Alpe di Siusi, enjoying hiking or mountain biking in Europe's largest high-altitude meadow. Have lunch at Gostner Schwaige, then continue exploring the scenic landscape. Return to

Selva di Val Gardena for dinner at a local pizzeria like Ristorante Pizzeria L'Muline.

Day 4: Exploring Cortina d'Ampezzo

Drive to Cortina d'Ampezzo, often referred to as the Queen of the Dolomites. Check into the luxurious Cristallo, a Luxury Collection Resort & Spa. Spend your day exploring the town's upscale shops and historic sites. Have lunch at Rifugio Scoiattoli, located on the Cinque Torri, offering both incredible views and hearty meals. In the afternoon, take the Faloria cable car for a panoramic view of the Ampezzo Valley. Conclude your day with dinner at El Toulà, a renowned restaurant offering traditional Italian cuisine with a modern twist.

Day 5: Departure

On your final day, enjoy a leisurely breakfast at your hotel. If time permits, visit the local markets in Cortina d'Ampezzo to pick up some regional delicacies. Return to Bolzano for your departure, ensuring you've captured the essence of the Dolomites' midweek escape.

Weeklong Adventure (7 Days or More)

A week in the Dolomites allows for a comprehensive exploration of the region's natural beauty, cultural landmarks, and culinary delights. This itinerary is designed to provide a rich and varied experience, from leisurely hikes to historical discoveries and indulgent dining.

Day 1: Arrival in Bolzano

Arrive in Bolzano, the gateway to the Dolomites, and check into Parkhotel Laurin, a historic hotel known for its elegant ambiance and central location. Spend the morning exploring Bolzano's historic center. Start with Piazza Walther, the city's bustling main square, where you can enjoy a coffee at one of the outdoor cafes while watching the lively activities. Visit the South Tyrol Museum of Archaeology to see the famous Ötzi the Iceman, a well-preserved mummy from the Copper Age. For lunch, try local South Tyrolean cuisine at Hopfen & Co., a popular brewery and restaurant. In the afternoon, take the Renon cable car for breathtaking views of the surrounding mountains. Enjoy a leisurely hike on the Renon Plateau, known for its serene landscapes and picturesque villages. Conclude your day with dinner at Restaurant Vögele, which offers a mix of traditional and modern dishes in a charming historical setting.

Day 2: Exploring Val Gardena

Drive to Val Gardena, one of the most picturesque valleys in the Dolomites. Check into Hotel Alpenroyal Grand Hotel Gourmet & Spa in Selva di Val Gardena, a luxurious choice for accommodation. Begin your exploration with a visit to the village of Ortisei. Stroll through its pedestrian-friendly center, admiring the colorful buildings and artisan shops. Have lunch at Tubladel, a cozy restaurant known for its delicious regional cuisine. In the afternoon, take the Seceda cable car up to the Seceda mountain, offering stunning panoramic views and numerous hiking trails. Return to Selva di Val Gardena for a relaxing evening, enjoying a gourmet dinner at the hotel's restaurant, which features a menu inspired by local and Mediterranean flavors.

Day 3: Adventure in Alpe di Siusi

Spend the day exploring Alpe di Siusi, the largest high-altitude Alpine meadow in Europe. The rolling meadows, dotted with traditional huts, provide an idyllic setting for a variety of activities. Enjoy a morning hike or mountain biking on the well-marked trails. For lunch, stop at Gostner Schwaige, a charming mountain hut renowned for its fresh, farm-to-table dishes. Try their homemade dumplings and other local specialties while enjoying the beautiful surroundings. In the afternoon, continue exploring the scenic landscape, taking in the stunning views of the surrounding peaks. Return to Selva di Val Gardena for dinner at a local pizzeria like Ristorante Pizzeria L'Muline, known for its wood-fired pizzas and cozy atmosphere.

Day 4: Discovering Cortina d'Ampezzo

Drive to Cortina d'Ampezzo, often referred to as the Queen of the Dolomites. Check into the luxurious Cristallo, a Luxury Collection Resort & Spa. Spend your day exploring the town's upscale shops and historic sites. Visit the Museo all'Aperto delle 5 Torri, an open-air museum dedicated to World War I history, set among the stunning Cinque Torri rock formations. Have lunch at Rifugio Scoiattoli, located on the Cinque Torri, offering both incredible views and hearty meals. In the afternoon, take the Faloria cable car for a panoramic view of the Ampezzo Valley. Conclude your day with dinner at El Toulà, a renowned restaurant offering traditional Italian cuisine with a modern twist.

Day 5: Hiking in the Tre Cime di Lavaredo

Spend the day hiking around the iconic Tre Cime di Lavaredo. Start your hike from Rifugio Auronzo, enjoying the stunning views of these majestic peaks. The trail around Tre Cime di Lavaredo is one of the most famous and scenic hikes in the Dolomites, offering spectacular views at every turn. Have lunch at Rifugio Locatelli, which provides a comfortable resting spot with delicious meals and breathtaking scenery. In the afternoon, continue your hike or explore the nearby trails that offer different perspectives of the Tre Cime. Return to Cortina d'Ampezzo for a relaxing evening and dinner at your hotel, reflecting on the day's adventures.

Day 6: Exploring Lake Braies

Drive to Lake Braies, one of the most beautiful lakes in the Dolomites. Enjoy a leisurely walk around the lake, capturing its stunning turquoise waters and surrounding mountains. The loop trail around Lake Braies is relatively easy and perfect for a relaxing morning. For lunch, dine at the Hotel Lago di Braies, a lakeside restaurant offering traditional Tyrolean dishes and a magnificent view of the lake. In the afternoon, you can rent a rowboat to explore the lake from the water, or visit the nearby Pragser Wildsee for more outdoor activities. Return to Cortina d'Ampezzo for dinner and relaxation, perhaps trying a different local restaurant to experience more of the region's culinary offerings.

Day 7: Departure

On your final day, enjoy a leisurely breakfast at your hotel in Cortina d'Ampezzo. If time permits, take a stroll through the town to visit any sights you may have missed, or do some last-minute shopping for souvenirs and local products. Drive back to Bolzano for your departure, ensuring you have ample time to return any rental equipment and prepare for your journey home. Reflect on the diverse experiences of your weeklong adventure in the Dolomites, from the cultural richness of Bolzano to the natural beauty of the alpine landscapes.

A weeklong adventure in the Dolomites offers a perfect blend of cultural exploration, outdoor activities, and culinary delights. By following this detailed itinerary, travelers can immerse themselves in the region's stunning landscapes and rich heritage, ensuring a memorable and enriching experience. Whether hiking through breathtaking mountain trails, exploring charming alpine villages, or savoring delicious local cuisine, the Dolomites provide a unique and unforgettable travel destination.

CHAPTER 8

PRACTICAL TIPS

Money Matters: Currency Exchange and Budgeting

Traveling to the Dolomites involves not just exploring stunning landscapes but also navigating the practicalities of managing money effectively. Understanding the local currency, where to exchange it, and how to budget can significantly enhance your travel experience.

The currency used in the Dolomites is the Euro (€), which is the official currency of Italy and most other European Union countries. Each Euro is subdivided into 100 cents, and coins and banknotes of various denominations are widely circulated. The Euro's stability and widespread acceptance make it convenient for travelers, ensuring seamless transactions throughout your stay in the Dolomites.

When it comes to exchanging currency, there are several options available in the Dolomites. Banks are a reliable choice, offering fair exchange rates and secure transactions. Most banks in the region have ATMs that accept international cards, allowing you to withdraw Euros directly. Exchange offices are another option, often found in tourist areas, but it's essential to compare their rates and fees, as they can vary widely. ATMs generally offer the most cost-effective exchange rates, but be mindful of any fees your home bank might charge for international withdrawals. It's advisable to inform your bank of your travel plans to avoid any issues with card usage abroad.

Budgeting Tips

Effective budgeting can make your trip to the Dolomites more enjoyable. Accommodation costs can vary significantly. For budget travelers, hostels and guesthouses can range from €30 to €60 per night. Mid-range hotels typically cost between €70 and €150 per night, while luxury accommodations can start at €200 and go up significantly depending on the amenities and location. Meals are another critical budget component. A budget traveler might spend around €10 to €15 for a meal at a casual eatery, while mid-range restaurants typically charge €20 to €40 per person. Fine dining experiences can cost upwards of €60 per person. Transportation costs, including buses and trains, are relatively affordable, with daily expenses ranging from €10 to €20. For activities, budget around €50 per day for entry fees, guided tours, and equipment rentals, though this can vary based on your interests and plans.

Payment Methods

Credit and debit cards are widely accepted throughout the Dolomites, especially in larger establishments, hotels, and restaurants. Visa and MasterCard are the most commonly accepted, but it's wise to carry some cash for smaller businesses, local markets, or rural areas where card payments may not be available. Contactless payment methods are also gaining popularity, so check if your bank card or mobile payment app is compatible. Having a mix of payment options ensures flexibility and convenience during your travels.

Local Pricing Insights

Pricing in the Dolomites can vary based on the season and location. Peak tourist seasons, such as summer and winter holidays, typically see higher prices for accommodation and activities. To save money, consider visiting during the shoulder seasons of spring and autumn, when prices are lower, and crowds are thinner. Tourist hotspots like Cortina d'Ampezzo or Bolzano tend to be more expensive than smaller, less frequented villages. Additionally, local markets and eateries offer more affordable options compared to tourist-centric restaurants and shops. Be aware of hidden costs such as city taxes, which are often added to hotel bills, and service charges in restaurants.

Resources and Tools

To manage your finances efficiently while traveling in the Dolomites, consider using budgeting apps like Mint or YNAB, which help track your spending and keep you within your budget. Currency converter apps such as XE Currency are invaluable for quickly converting prices and understanding costs in your home currency. Websites like TripAdvisor and local travel forums offer up-to-date insights on costs and recommendations for budget-friendly dining and accommodation options. These tools can help you stay on top of your finances and make informed decisions throughout your trip.

Managing money effectively in the Dolomites involves understanding the local currency, finding cost-effective exchange options, and budgeting wisely across different categories. By planning ahead, using a mix of payment methods, and taking advantage of digital tools, you can enjoy a memorable and financially smooth trip to this breathtaking region.

Safety and Health: Staying Safe in the Dolomites

The Dolomites, with their stunning landscapes and myriad outdoor activities, offer a perfect destination for adventure and relaxation. To make the most of your trip and ensure your well-being, it's essential to prioritize safety and health. Here's a comprehensive guide to staying safe and healthy while exploring this beautiful region.

General Safety Tips

When traveling in the Dolomites, it's important to stay aware of your surroundings at all times. Although the area is generally safe, it's wise to avoid secluded areas, especially at night, and keep your valuables secure. Respect local customs and traditions, as the Dolomites have a rich cultural heritage that locals take pride in. Learning a few basic Italian phrases can also enhance your experience and help you in everyday interactions. Always follow local regulations and guidelines, especially when it comes to environmental conservation and wildlife protection.

Outdoor Safety

The Dolomites are renowned for their outdoor activities, from hiking and skiing to climbing. Before setting out, always check the weather forecast as conditions can change rapidly in mountainous regions. Ensure you understand trail markers and difficulty levels to avoid getting lost or venturing onto paths beyond your skill level. Carry a detailed map and a compass, even if you plan to use GPS, as signal can be unreliable in remote areas. Recognize the symptoms of altitude sickness, which include headaches, dizziness, and nausea, and descend to a lower altitude if they occur. For skiing, always wear appropriate gear, stay on marked slopes, and be aware of avalanche risks.

Health Precautions

Staying healthy in the Dolomites requires some basic precautions. Hydration is key, especially when engaging in physical activities. Carry a reusable water bottle and drink regularly. Use sunscreen with a high SPF to protect against UV rays, which can be intense at higher altitudes, and reapply throughout the day. Dressing in layers is crucial to adapt to changing weather conditions; mornings and evenings can be chilly even in summer. In winter, proper thermal clothing is essential to prevent hypothermia. There are no specific vaccinations required for the Dolomites, but it's always wise to be up-to-date with routine immunizations and check for any health advisories before traveling.

Language and Communication: Essential Phrases

Traveling to the Dolomites offers a unique opportunity to experience a region rich in cultural diversity. One of the best ways to connect with the local community is through language. Here's a comprehensive guide to help you navigate language and communication during your visit to the Dolomites.

The Dolomites, straddling Italy's northern border, are a linguistic mosaic where both Italian and German are commonly spoken. In the provinces of South Tyrol and Trentino, German holds significant sway due to historical influences, while Italian is the predominant language in Veneto and other parts of Trentino-Alto Adige. You may also encounter Ladin, a Rhaeto-Romance language spoken by a small community in the central Dolomites. This linguistic diversity enriches the cultural fabric of the region and provides travelers with a unique experience.

Basic Greetings and Polite Phrases

Mastering a few basic greetings and polite phrases can go a long way in enhancing your travel experience. Here are essential phrases in both Italian and German, along with phonetic pronunciations:

Hello: *Italian - Ciao (chow), German - Hallo (hah-loh)*

Please: *Italian - Per favore (pehr fah-voh-reh), German - Bitte (bi-teh)*

Thank you: *Italian - Grazie (grah-tsyeh), German - Danke (dahn-keh)*

Excuse me: *Italian - Scusi (skoo-zee), German - Entschuldigung (ent-shool-dee-goong)*

Good morning: *Italian - Buongiorno (bwohn-jor-noh), German - Guten Morgen (goo-ten mor-gen)*

Good evening: *Italian - Buonasera (bwohn-ah-seh-rah), German - Guten Abend (goo-ten ah-bent)*

Useful Phrases for Travelers

Navigating various travel situations is easier with a handy set of phrases. Here are some practical phrases for different scenarios:

Ordering Food: *Italian - Vorrei ordinare... (vor-ray or-dee-nah-reh...), German - Ich möchte bestellen... (eekh merkh-teh bes-tel-len...)*

Asking for Directions: *Italian - Dove si trova...? (doh-veh see troh-vah...), German - Wo befindet sich...? (voh be-fin-det zik...)*

Making Purchases: *Italian - Quanto costa? (kwahn-toh koh-stah?), German - Wie viel kostet das? (vee feel koss-tet dahs?)*

Seeking Assistance: *Italian - Mi può aiutare? (mee pwoh ah-yoo-tah-reh?), German - Können Sie mir helfen? (kuh-nen zee meer hel-fen?)*

Language Learning Resources

Preparing for your trip with some language learning can make a significant difference. Here are a few recommended resources tailored for travelers to the Dolomites:

Mobile Apps: Duolingo, Babbel, and Rosetta Stone offer Italian and German courses that are interactive and easy to use.
Online Tutorials: Websites like FluentU and BBC Languages provide free resources and tutorials for learning basic phrases in Italian and German.

Cultural Insights

Understanding cultural nuances in communication can greatly enhance your interactions. In the Dolomites, formality in language is important. For instance, using "Lei" (lay) in Italian or "Sie" (zee) in German to address someone formally shows respect. Informal forms like "tu" (too) in Italian and "du" (doo) in German are reserved for friends and family. Additionally, body language and eye contact are key; making eye contact shows attentiveness and respect. It's also polite to greet people when entering shops or restaurants with a simple "Buongiorno" or "Guten Morgen."

Multilingual Assistance

The Dolomites are well-prepared for international visitors. Many staff members at major tourist attractions, hotels, and restaurants speak English. Signs and menus are often available in multiple languages, including English, Italian, and German. If you need assistance, look for information desks or tourist offices where multilingual staff can help with directions and recommendations.

Respect and Appreciation

Learning and using basic phrases in Italian and German demonstrates respect and appreciation for the local culture. Even a simple "Grazie" or "Danke" can create a positive connection with locals. It shows that you value their language and are making an effort to engage. This small gesture can enhance your travel experience, making interactions more meaningful and memorable.

Embracing the linguistic diversity of the Dolomites can greatly enrich your travel experience. By learning essential phrases, understanding cultural nuances, and utilizing available resources, you can communicate effectively and build deeper connections with the local community. Enjoy the beautiful blend of languages and cultures that the Dolomites have to offer.

Emergency Contacts

In case of an emergency, knowing the right contacts can be lifesaving. The general emergency number in Italy is 112, which connects you to all emergency services including police, fire brigade, and medical assistance. For outdoor rescue services specific to the Dolomites, you can dial 118. It's also useful to have the contact details of local hospitals and clinics. Major hospitals in the region include the Bolzano Central Hospital and the Trento Hospital. Additionally, keeping a list of nearby pharmacies and their operating hours can be very helpful for non-emergency health issues.

Travel Insurance

Obtaining comprehensive travel insurance is crucial for any trip, particularly when visiting the Dolomites with its range of outdoor activities. Look for a policy that covers medical expenses, emergency evacuations, and activities such as skiing and hiking. Make sure your insurance also covers trip cancellations or interruptions, lost or stolen belongings, and personal liability. Having travel insurance provides peace of mind and financial protection in case of unexpected incidents.

Local Health Services

Healthcare in the Dolomites is generally of high quality. Pharmacies are well-stocked with medications and health supplies, and pharmacists can often provide advice and minor health consultations. For more serious health issues, local clinics and hospitals are equipped to handle emergencies and provide necessary care. It's useful to note that many healthcare providers in tourist areas speak English, but learning some basic Italian medical terms can still be helpful. Always carry a copy of your health insurance information and identification.

Resources and Tools

Staying informed and prepared can significantly enhance your safety and health while traveling. Download safety apps such as "Emergency App" which provides information and alerts for natural disasters and emergency situations. Websites like "Visit Dolomites" offer up-to-date information on trail conditions, weather forecasts, and safety tips. Guides and maps from local tourist offices can also provide valuable insights and recommendations. Joining local hiking or skiing groups can offer additional safety and companionship.

Prioritizing safety and health while traveling in the Dolomites ensures a memorable and enjoyable experience. By following these guidelines, staying informed, and taking necessary precautions, you can fully immerse yourself in the beauty and adventure of this incredible region.

Emergency Phone Numbers

Familiarizing yourself with key emergency phone numbers is crucial for a safe trip. The general emergency number in Italy is 112, which connects you to all emergency services. For specific needs, you can directly contact the Carabinieri (local police) at 113, ambulance services at 118, the fire department at 115, and mountain rescue services at 144. In the Dolomites, the Aiut Alpin Dolomites can be reached at+39 0471 836500, providing specialized mountain rescue services. These numbers are staffed by multilingual operators, but it's helpful to know basic Italian or German phrases to communicate your situation clearly.

Local Hospitals and Clinics

Several hospitals and clinics are available in key towns throughout the Dolomites. In Bolzano, the main hospital is Azienda Sanitaria dell'Alto Adige (South Tyrol Health Authority), located at Via Lorenz Boehler 5, contact number +39 0471 909000. In Cortina d'Ampezzo, the Ospedale di Cortina is located at Via Majon di Sopra 16, contact number+39 0436 883111. For Val Gardena, the nearest facility is the Ospedale di Bressanone at Via Dante 52, Bressanone, contact number +39 0472 813111. These hospitals offer comprehensive medical services, including emergency care, and have English-speaking staff available.

What to Do in an Emergency

In case of an emergency, immediately dial 112. Clearly state your location, the nature of the emergency, and any injuries or immediate dangers. If language barriers arise, operators often speak multiple languages, but having basic knowledge of key phrases in Italian or German can be beneficial. When providing information, mention landmarks or coordinates if you're in a remote area. If involved in an outdoor activity, knowing the trail or area name helps emergency responders locate you quickly.

Travel Insurance and Assistance

Travel insurance is a crucial safety net for any trip, especially in a region with adventurous activities like the Dolomites. Ensure your travel insurance covers medical emergencies, evacuations, and outdoor activities like hiking and skiing. Most insurance companies offer emergency assistance services, including 24/7 hotlines and medical evacuation coordination. Before your trip, familiarize yourself with your policy's emergency procedures and keep a copy of your insurance details handy.

Personal Safety Tips

When engaging in outdoor activities, preparation is key to safety. Always carry a well-stocked first aid kit, sufficient water, and weather-appropriate clothing. Inform someone of your plans, especially when hiking or skiing in remote areas. Check weather forecasts and trail conditions before setting out, and be aware of the signs of altitude sickness. Having a map, compass, and a fully charged mobile phone can be lifesavers in case of an emergency.

Cultural Considerations

Understanding local customs and cultural nuances can aid in navigating emergency situations more effectively. Italians and Germans in the Dolomites value politeness and clear communication. When seeking help from locals, a friendly and respectful approach goes a long way. Using phrases like "Per favore" (please) and "Grazie" (thank you) shows respect and can make interactions smoother. In rural areas, locals are often familiar with the terrain and can offer invaluable assistance.

Resources and Tools

Several resources can help travelers stay prepared for emergencies. Apps like First Aid by the Red Cross offer crucial information on handling medical emergencies. The website of the Italian National Alpine Rescue Corps (www.cnsas.it) provides detailed safety advice and contact information. Keeping a digital copy of local emergency numbers and addresses of nearby hospitals on your phone can be incredibly useful.

Preparing for emergencies in the Dolomites involves knowing key contact numbers, understanding how to communicate effectively, and being aware of local resources. By following these guidelines, travelers can ensure a safer and more enjoyable trip, ready to handle any unexpected situations with confidence.

Best Photography Spots in the Dolomites

The Dolomites, with their striking landscapes and enchanting vistas, offer a myriad of breathtaking photography opportunities. Each spot presents a unique aspect of the region's natural beauty, making it a paradise for photographers seeking to capture stunning images. Here's a guide to some of the best photography locations in the Dolomites, each providing a different perspective of this extraordinary landscape.

1. Tre Cime di Lavaredo

The Tre Cime di Lavaredo, or Three Peaks, is a quintessential image of the Dolomites. These three imposing peaks rise dramatically against the sky, their jagged profiles creating a striking contrast with the surrounding alpine scenery. The classic view of these peaks can be captured from the Rifugio Auronzo area, where you'll find a trail that encircles the peaks, offering various vantage points.

To reach Tre Cime di Lavaredo, drive from Cortina d'Ampezzo to the Rifugio Auronzo parking lot, which takes about 45 minutes and involves a scenic drive through the mountains. Alternatively, local buses operate from Cortina to the parking area. From Rifugio Auronzo, a well-marked path provides access to some of the most photogenic spots. The peaks look particularly dramatic during the early morning or late afternoon, when the light accentuates their rugged features and casts long shadows over the landscape.

2. Lago di Braies (Pragser Wildsee)

Lago di Braies is renowned for its enchanting emerald waters and picturesque mountain backdrop. The lake's calm, mirror-like surface often reflects the surrounding peaks, creating an almost surreal image that is a photographer's dream. The best shots are usually captured in the early morning, when the water is at its calmest and the reflections are most striking.

To get to Lago di Braies, drive from Cortina d'Ampezzo, which takes around 40 minutes. Parking is available near the lake, but if you're relying on public transport, take a train to the nearby town and then a local bus or taxi to the lake. The serene morning light and the tranquil atmosphere make this spot ideal for capturing beautiful and serene photographs.

3. Seceda

Seceda, with its sweeping meadows and dramatic ridges, offers panoramic views of the Dolomites that are perfect for wide-angle shots. The distinctive green meadows contrasted with the rugged mountain ridges provide a unique perspective that changes throughout the day with the shifting light.

To access Seceda, take the cable car from Ortisei, which provides stunning views as you ascend. Ortisei is accessible by train and bus from Bolzano. Once at Seceda, explore the area and take advantage of the varied perspectives and expansive views. The best times for photography are during sunrise or sunset when the light adds depth and warmth to the landscape.

4. Alpe di Siusi (Seiser Alm)

Alpe di Siusi, or Seiser Alm, is the largest high-altitude plateau in Europe and offers breathtaking views of rolling meadows set against a backdrop of towering peaks. The plateau's vast expanse and the interplay of light and shadow make it an excellent location for capturing wide, sweeping landscapes.

To reach Alpe di Siusi, ride the cable car from Ortisei, which provides scenic views as you travel up to the plateau. The area is a short walk from the cable car station. The expansive meadows and panoramic views are best photographed during the golden hours of sunrise or sunset, when the soft light enhances the colors and textures of the landscape.

5. Lago di Sorapis

Lago di Sorapis is famous for its striking turquoise waters, framed by rugged mountain peaks. The lake's unique color and the dramatic setting create a stunning visual contrast, making it a prime spot for capturing vibrant and eye-catching images.

To reach Lago di Sorapis, hike from the Passo Tre Croci. The trailhead is accessible by car or bus from Cortina d'Ampezzo. If you're not driving, take a bus to Passo Tre Croci and follow the well-marked trail to the lake. The vibrant color of the water is most vivid on sunny days, and the rugged peaks surrounding the lake add a dramatic element to your photographs.

These photography spots in the Dolomites each offer a unique way to experience and capture the region's stunning beauty. From the iconic Tre Cime di Lavaredo to the serene reflections at Lago di Braies, the Dolomites provide a wealth of opportunities for creating memorable and striking images.

Useful Apps for Your Journey to the Dolomites

Traveling to the Dolomites offers a blend of stunning landscapes, outdoor adventures, and cultural richness. Leveraging the right apps can significantly enhance your travel experience, from planning and navigation to communication and safety. Here's a detailed guide to the most essential apps for your journey to the Dolomites.

Several apps are indispensable for planning and navigating your trip to the Dolomites. For transportation, Rome2Rio and Trenitalia provide comprehensive options for getting around. Accommodation apps like Booking.com and Airbnb offer diverse lodging choices. For outdoor activities, apps like AllTrails and Gaia GPS are invaluable for exploring the mountains. These apps collectively ensure a seamless travel experience, covering all aspects from logistics to leisure.

Hiking and Outdoor Apps

The Dolomites are renowned for their hiking trails and outdoor adventures. AllTrails is an excellent app for finding and mapping hiking routes. It offers user reviews, trail maps, and difficulty ratings. Gaia GPS is another robust tool for outdoor navigation, providing detailed topographic maps and offline capabilities. ViewRanger is ideal for those looking for advanced route planning and real-time navigation. These apps not only help in planning hikes but also ensure safety by providing up-to-date trail information and weather forecasts.

Accommodation and Dining Apps

Finding the perfect place to stay and dine in the Dolomites is made easier with apps like Booking.com and Airbnb. These platforms allow you to compare prices, read reviews, and book accommodations that suit your preferences. For dining, TripAdvisor is an excellent resource for finding top-rated restaurants, cafes, and local eateries. With these apps, you can seamlessly book a cozy mountain lodge or a gourmet dining experience, ensuring comfort and satisfaction throughout your stay.

Language and Translation Apps

Communicating with locals and navigating the Dolomites is simplified with language and translation apps. Google Translate is a versatile tool for translating text, voice, and even images of menus and signs. Duolingo is great for learning basic Italian and German phrases, offering a fun and interactive way to practice. iTranslate provides robust translation capabilities and offline mode, crucial for areas with limited internet access. These apps help bridge the language gap, making interactions smoother and more enjoyable.

Emergency and Safety Apps

Safety is paramount when traveling, and having the right apps can be a lifesaver. The First Aid app by the American Red Cross offers step-by-step instructions for handling medical emergencies. GeoSure Travel Safety provides real-time safety ratings for various locations, helping you stay informed about local conditions. Travel insurance apps from providers like World Nomads offer quick access to emergency assistance and claims services. These apps ensure you are prepared for any unexpected situations, providing peace of mind during your travels.

Cultural and Historical Apps

Exploring the cultural and historical aspects of the Dolomites is enhanced with specialized apps. Dolomiti UNESCO offers insights into the natural and cultural heritage of the region, including walking tours and historical facts. Dolomiti Superski is perfect for winter sports enthusiasts, providing information on ski slopes, weather conditions, and lift passes. These apps enrich your travel experience, offering deeper connections to the region's heritage and attractions.

Offline Capabilities

Given the remote nature of some areas in the Dolomites, having apps with offline capabilities is crucial. Download maps and guides from apps like Google Maps and Gaia GPS beforehand to ensure you have access to essential information without internet connectivity. This preparation ensures you can navigate and explore even in the most secluded parts of the Dolomites, maintaining safety and convenience.

Tips for Downloading and Using Apps

To make the most of these apps, ensure your devices are fully charged and carry a backup power source, like a portable charger. Be mindful of data usage and consider downloading necessary content and maps before traveling to avoid roaming charges. Regularly update apps to access the latest features and improvements. Familiarize yourself with app interfaces before your trip to ensure smooth usage during your travels.

By integrating these apps into your travel plans, you can enhance every aspect of your journey to the Dolomites, from preparation and navigation to safety and cultural exploration. These tools make it easier to focus on enjoying the breathtaking landscapes and unique experiences that the Dolomites have to offer.

MAP

Scan QR Code with device to view map for easy navigation

CONCLUSION

Reflecting on the unique aspects of the Dolomites, it becomes clear why this region is a special destination for travelers. The Dolomites offer a harmonious blend of natural beauty, outdoor adventures, rich culture, and culinary delights. The towering peaks and serene valleys provide a breathtaking backdrop for activities like hiking, skiing, and climbing, while the charming villages and towns introduce visitors to the local culture and traditions. The diverse culinary scene, featuring hearty Tyrolean dishes and refined Italian cuisine, adds to the sensory pleasures of exploring this region. Every aspect of the Dolomites, from its pristine landscapes to its vibrant festivals, contributes to an enriching and unforgettable travel experience.

Encouraging readers to embrace the Dolomite experience, I recall my first visit to the region. The moment I laid eyes on the jagged peaks bathed in the warm glow of the setting sun, I felt an overwhelming sense of wonder and adventure. Engaging with locals, tasting regional specialties like speck and canederli, and hiking through the breathtaking trails of the Alpe di Siusi left an indelible mark on me. The Dolomites inspire a deep appreciation for nature's grandeur and the simple joys of life. This personal connection is a testament to the region's power to captivate and inspire every traveler.

Stepping outside one's comfort zone is an essential part of the Dolomite experience. Whether it's hiking a challenging trail like the Via Ferrata, tasting unique local dishes, or engaging with the local culture during a traditional festival, the rewards of these experiences are immeasurable. Trying new activities and immersing oneself in the local way of life can lead to profound personal growth and unforgettable memories. The Dolomites invite you to embrace the spirit of adventure and discover the joy of exploring new horizons.

While the popular tourist spots in the Dolomites are undoubtedly worth visiting, venturing beyond these attractions often leads to the most memorable moments. Exploring lesser-known areas, hidden gems, and local traditions can provide a deeper understanding of the region's culture and natural beauty. Whether it's discovering a secluded alpine meadow, attending a village festival, or hiking a lesser-traveled trail, these experiences enrich your journey and offer unique insights into the Dolomites. Embrace the opportunity to explore beyond the beaten path and uncover the true essence of this remarkable region.

Made in United States
Orlando, FL
10 December 2024